ESSENTIAL GUITAR LIBRARY
THE GREAT AMERICAN SONGBOOK

Cover photo:
Gibson Limited Historic 1934 L-5 courtesy of Gibson Guitars

Alfred Publishing Co., Inc.
16320 Roscoe Blvd., Suite 100
P.O. Box 10003
Van Nuys, CA 91410-0003
alfred.com

Copyright © MMVII by Alfred Publishing Co., Inc.
All rights reserved. Printed in USA.

ISBN-10: 0-7390-4512-1
ISBN-13: 978-0-7390-4512-1

CONTENTS

TITLE	COMPOSER	PAGE
ALL OF YOU	Cole Porter	4
AM I BLUE?	Akst/Clarke	5
ANYTHING GOES	Cole Porter	6
AS TIME GOES BY	Herman Hupfeld	8
AT LAST	Warren/Gordon	9
BEGIN THE BEGUINE	Cole Porter	10
THE BEST THINGS IN LIFE ARE FREE	Desylva/Brown/Henderson	12
BEWITCHED (Bothered and Bewildered)	Rodgers/Hart	13
BLUE MOON	Rodgers/Hart	14
BUT NOT FOR ME	Gershwin/Gershwin	15
COME FLY WITH ME	Van Heusen/Cahn	16
DO NOTHIN' TILL YOU HEAR FROM ME	Ellington/Russell	18
DON'T GET AROUND MUCH ANYMORE	Ellington/Russell	19
EMBRACEABLE YOU	Gershwin/Gershwin	24
A FOGGY DAY	Gershwin/Gershwin	20
I CAN'T GET STARTED	Duke/Gershwin	22
I COULD WRITE A BOOK	Rodgers/Hart	25
I GET A KICK OUT OF YOU	Cole Porter	26
I GOT RHYTHM	Gershwin/Gershwin	30
I ONLY HAVE EYES FOR YOU	Warren/Dubin	28
I WANNA BE AROUND (To Pick Up the Pieces)	Johnny Mercer	31
I'LL BE SEEING YOU	Fain/Kahal	32
I'LL SEE YOU IN MY DREAMS	Jones/Kahn	33
I'M IN THE MOOD FOR LOVE	McHugh/Fields	34
IT HAD TO BE YOU	Kahn/Jones	39
I'VE GOT A CRUSH ON YOU	Gershwin/Gershwin	35
I'VE GOT YOU UNDER MY SKIN	Cole Porter	36

TITLE	COMPOSER	PAGE
I'VE GROWN ACCUSTOMED TO HER FACE	Lerner/Loewe	38
THE LADY IS A TRAMP	Rodgers/Hart	40
LAURA	Raksin/Mercer	46
LET'S DO IT (Let's Fall in Love)	Cole Porter	42
LOVE FOR SALE	Cole Porter	44
LOVE IS HERE TO STAY	Gershwin/Gershwin	47
MOONGLOW	Hudson/De Lange/Mills	48
MORE THAN YOU KNOW	Eliscu/Rose/Youmans	49
MY FUNNY VALENTINE	Rodgers/Hart	56
NEVERTHELESS (I'm in Love with You)	Kalmar/Ruby	50
NIGHT AND DAY	Cole Porter	52
OVER THE RAINBOW	Arlen/Harburg	54
PENNIES FROM HEAVEN	Johnston/Burke	57
'S WONDERFUL	Gershwin/Gershwin	58
SATIN DOLL	Ellington/Strayhorn/Mercer	59
SKYLARK	Carmichael/Mercer	60
SOMEONE TO WATCH OVER ME	Gershwin/Gershwin	66
STAR DUST	Carmichael/Parish	62
STORMY WEATHER (Keeps Rainin' All the Time)	Koehler/Arlen	64
SUMMER WIND	Bradtke/Meier/Mercer	67
SUMMERTIME	Gershwin/Gershwin/Heyward/Heyward	72
THEY CAN'T TAKE THAT AWAY FROM ME	Gershwin/Gershwin	68
WHAT A WONDERFUL WORLD	Weiss/Thiele	70
WHAT'S NEW?	Haggart/Burke	73
WHEN I FALL IN LOVE	Young/Heyman	78
WHERE OR WHEN	Rodgers/Hart	74
YOU GO TO MY HEAD	Coots/Gillespie	76

CONTENTS BY COMPOSER

Akst/Clarke
AM I BLUE? 5

Arlen/Harburg
OVER THE RAINBOW 54

Bradtke/Meier/Mercer
SUMMER WIND 67

Carmichael/Mercer
SKYLARK 60
STAR DUST 62

Coots/Gillespie
YOU GO TO MY HEAD 76

Desylva/Brown/Henderson
THE BEST THINGS IN LIFE ARE FREE 12

Duke/Gershwin
I CAN'T GET STARTED 22

Eliscu/Rose/Youmans
MORE THAN YOU KNOW 49

Ellington/Russell
DO NOTHIN' TILL YOU HEAR FROM ME 18
DON'T GET AROUND MUCH ANYMORE 19

Ellington/Strayhorn/Mercer
SATIN DOLL 59

Fain/Kahal
I'LL BE SEEING YOU 32

Gershwin/Gershwin
BUT NOT FOR ME 15
EMBRACEABLE YOU 24
A FOGGY DAY 20
I GOT RHYTHM 30
I'VE GOT A CRUSH ON YOU 35
LOVE IS HERE TO STAY 47
'S WONDERFUL 58
SOMEONE TO WATCH OVER ME 66
THEY CAN'T TAKE THAT AWAY
  FROM ME 68

Gershwin/Gershwin/Heyward/Heyward
SUMMERTIME 72

Haggart/Burke
WHAT'S NEW? 73

Hudson/De Lange/Mills
MOONGLOW 48

Herman Hupfeld
AS TIME GOES BY 8

Jones/Kahn
I'LL SEE YOU IN MY DREAMS 33
IT HAD TO BE YOU 39

Kalmar/Ruby
NEVERTHELESS (I'M IN LOVE WITH YOU) 50

Koehler/Arlen
STORMY WEATHER 64

Lerner/Loewe
I'VE GROWN ACCUSTOMED TO
  HER FACE 38

McHugh/Fields
I'M IN THE MOOD FOR LOVE 34

Johnny Mercer
I WANNA BE AROUND (TO PICK UP
  THE PIECES) 31

Johnston/Burke
PENNIES FROM HEAVEN 57

Cole Porter
ALL OF YOU 4
ANYTHING GOES 6
BEGIN THE BEGUINE 10
I GET A KICK OUT OF YOU 26
I'VE GOT YOU UNDER MY SKIN 36
LET'S DO IT (LET'S FALL IN LOVE) 42
LOVE FOR SALE 44
NIGHT AND DAY 52

Raksin/Mercer
LAURA 46

Rodgers/Hart
BEWITCHED (BOTHERED AND BEWILDERED) 13
BLUE MOON 14
I COULD WRITE A BOOK 25
THE LADY IS A TRAMP 40
MY FUNNY VALENTINE 56
WHERE OR WHEN 74

Van Heusen/Cahn
COME FLY WITH ME 16

Warren/Dubin
I ONLY HAVE EYES FOR YOU 28

Warren/Gordon
AT LAST 9

Weiss/Thiele
WHAT A WONDERFUL WORLD 70

Young/Heyman
WHEN I FALL IN LOVE 78

ALL OF YOU

Music and Lyrics by
COLE PORTER

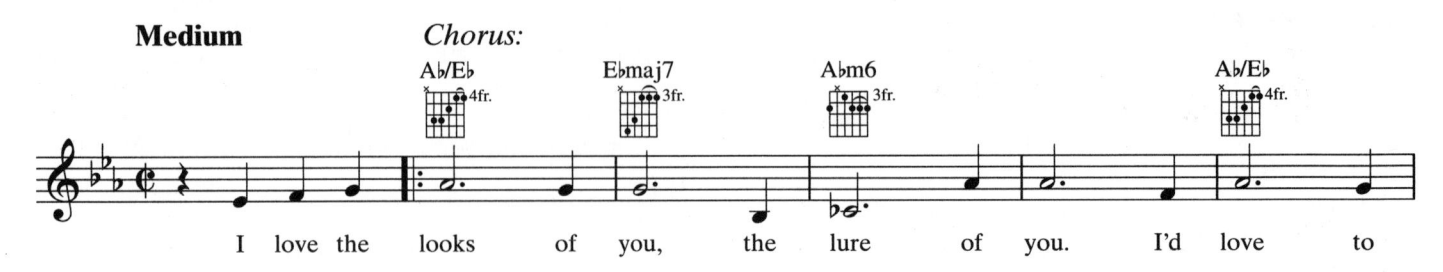

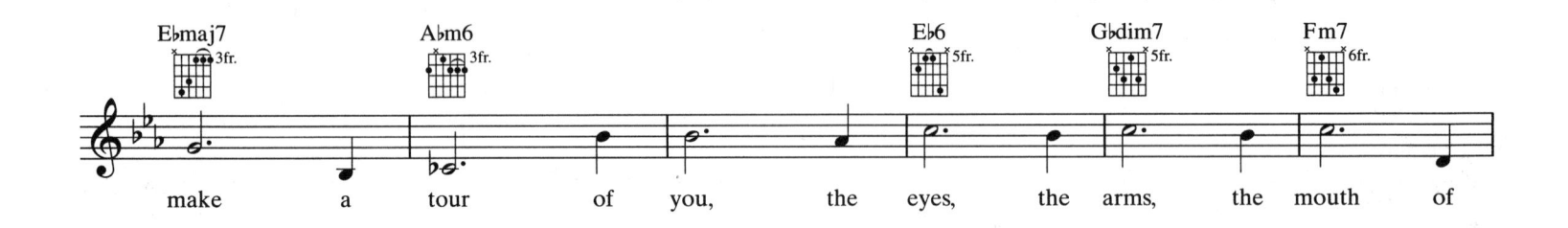

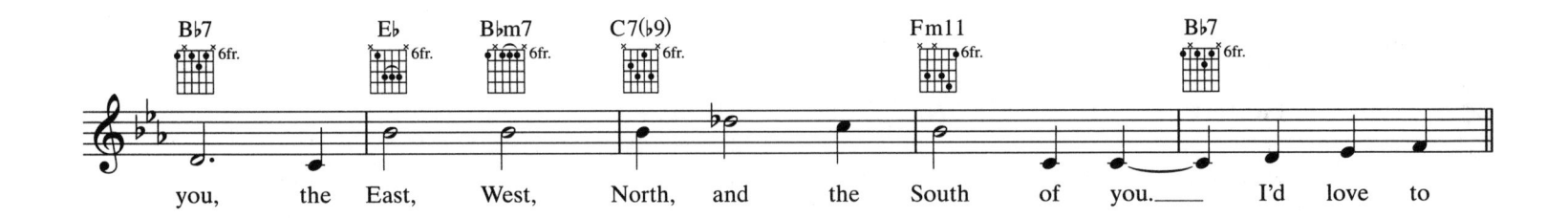

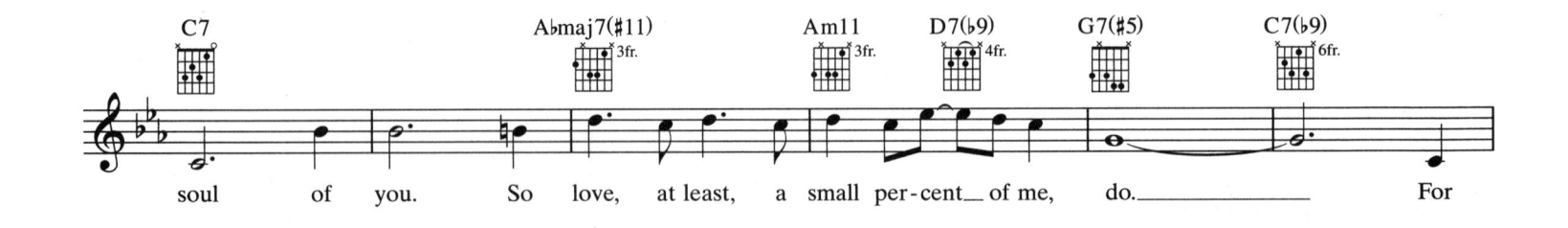

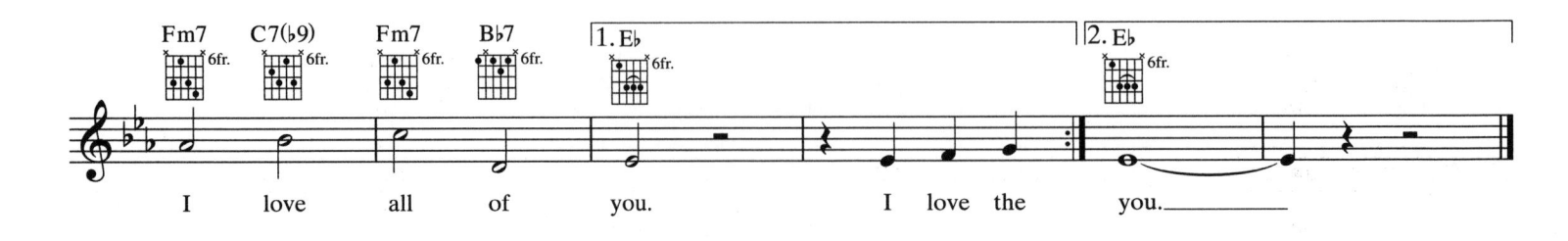

Medium *Chorus:*

I love the looks of you, the lure of you. I'd love to make a tour of you, the eyes, the arms, the mouth of you, the East, West, North, and the South of you. I'd love to gain com-plete con-trol of you, and han-dle e-ven the heart and soul of you. So love, at least, a small per-cent of me, do. For

1. I love all of you.

2. I love the you.

© 1954 by COLE PORTER (Renewed)
Chappell & Co., owner of publication and allied rights throughout the World
All Rights Reserved

AM I BLUE?

Lyric by GRANT CLARKE
Music by HARRY AKST

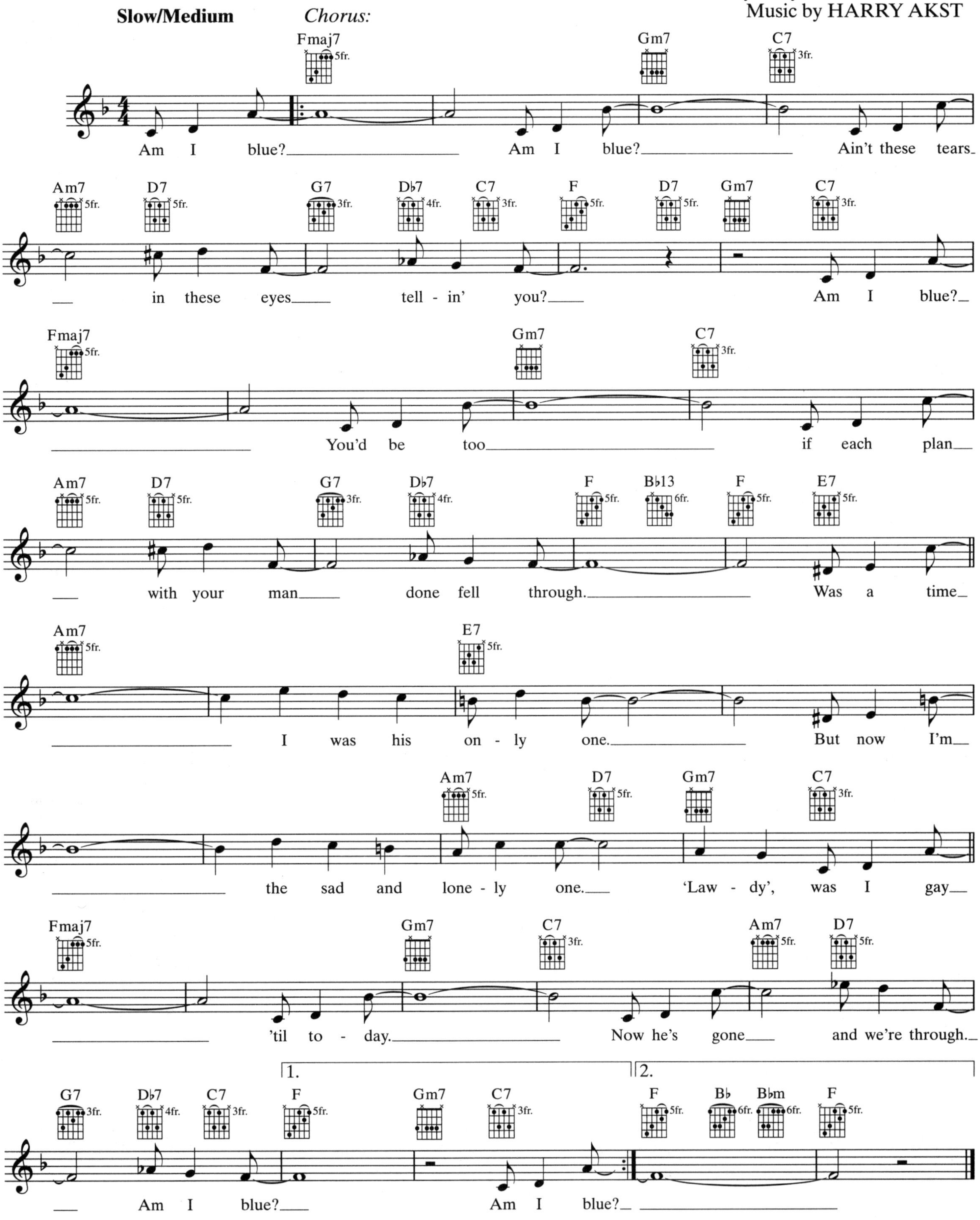

ANYTHING GOES

Music and Lyrics by
COLE PORTER

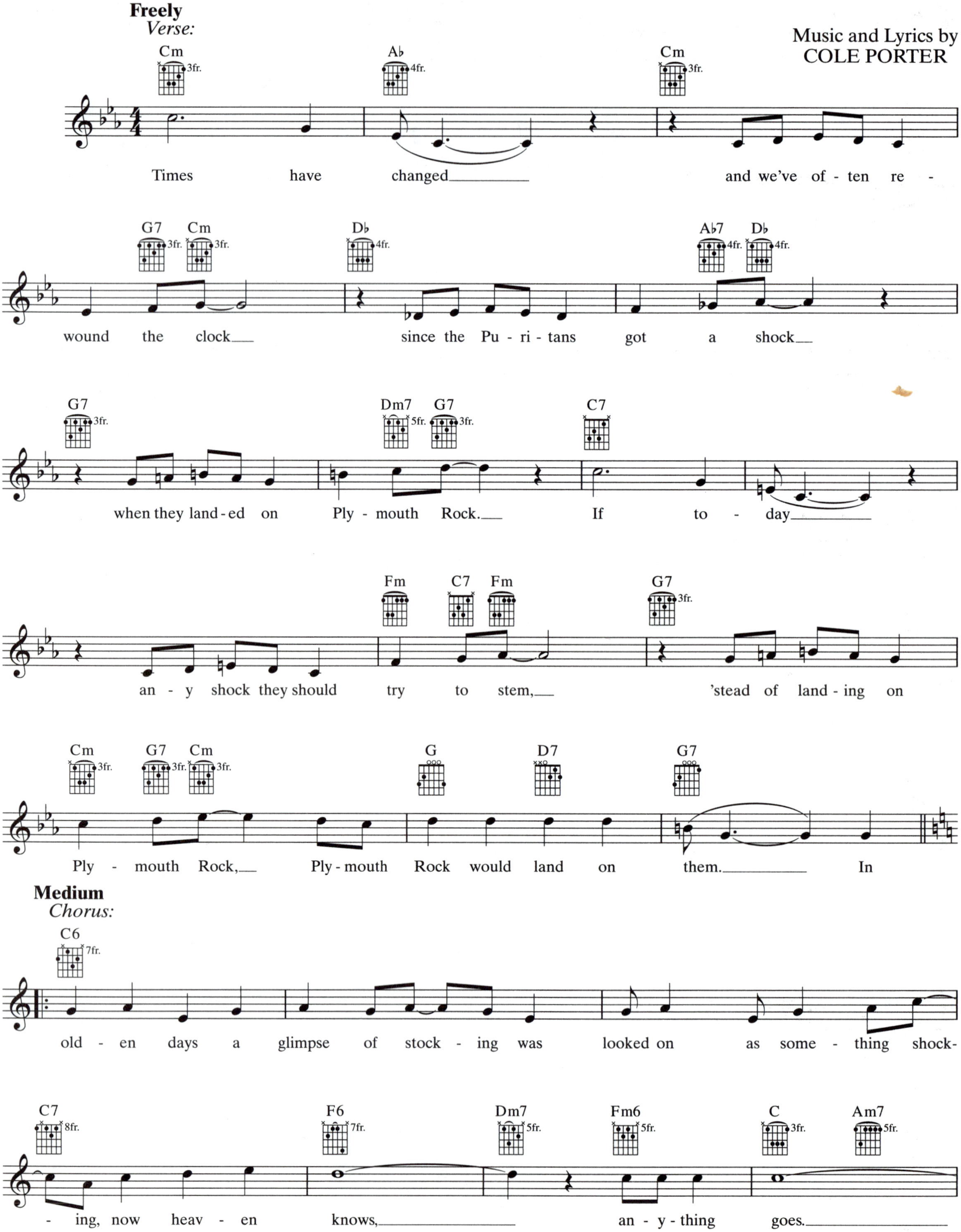

Dm7 5fr. G7 3fr. C6 7fr.
— Good au - thors to who once knew bet - ter words now on - ly use four - let -
C7 8fr. F6 7fr. Dm7 5fr. Fm6 5fr. C 3fr.
- ter words writ - ing prose, an - y - thing goes.
B7 7fr. Emaj7 7fr. F♯m7 9fr. B7 7fr.
The world has gone mad to - day. And good's bad to - day. And black's
E7 7fr. B7 7fr. Em7 7fr.
white to - day. And day's night to - day. When most guys to - day, that wom - en
Em7/D 7fr. C♯dim7 3fr. G13 3fr.
prize to - day, are just sil - ly gig - o - los. So
C6 7fr.
though I'm not a great ro - manc - er I know that (you're) bound to an -
(I'm)
C7 8fr. F6 7fr. Dm7 5fr. Dm7/G 5fr.
- swer when (I) pro - pose, an - y - thing
(you)
1. C 3fr.
goes. In
2. C 3fr. G11 3fr. C 3fr.
goes.

AS TIME GOES BY

Freely or Ballad

Chorus:

Words and Music by
HERMAN HUPFELD

You must re-mem-ber this, a kiss is still a kiss, a sigh is just a sigh; the fun-da-men-tal things ap-ply, as time goes by. And when two lov-ers woo, they still say, 'I love you,' on that you can re-ly; no mat-ter what the fu-ture brings, as time goes by. Moon-light and love songs nev-er out of date, hearts full of pas-sion, jea-lous-y and hate; wom-an needs man and man must have his mate, that no man can de-ny. It's still the same old sto-ry, a fight for love and glo-ry, a case of do or die! The world will al-ways wel-come lov-ers as time goes by. You by.

© 1931 WARNER BROS. INC. (Renewed)
All Rights Reserved

AT LAST

Music by HARRY WARREN
Lyric by MACK GORDON

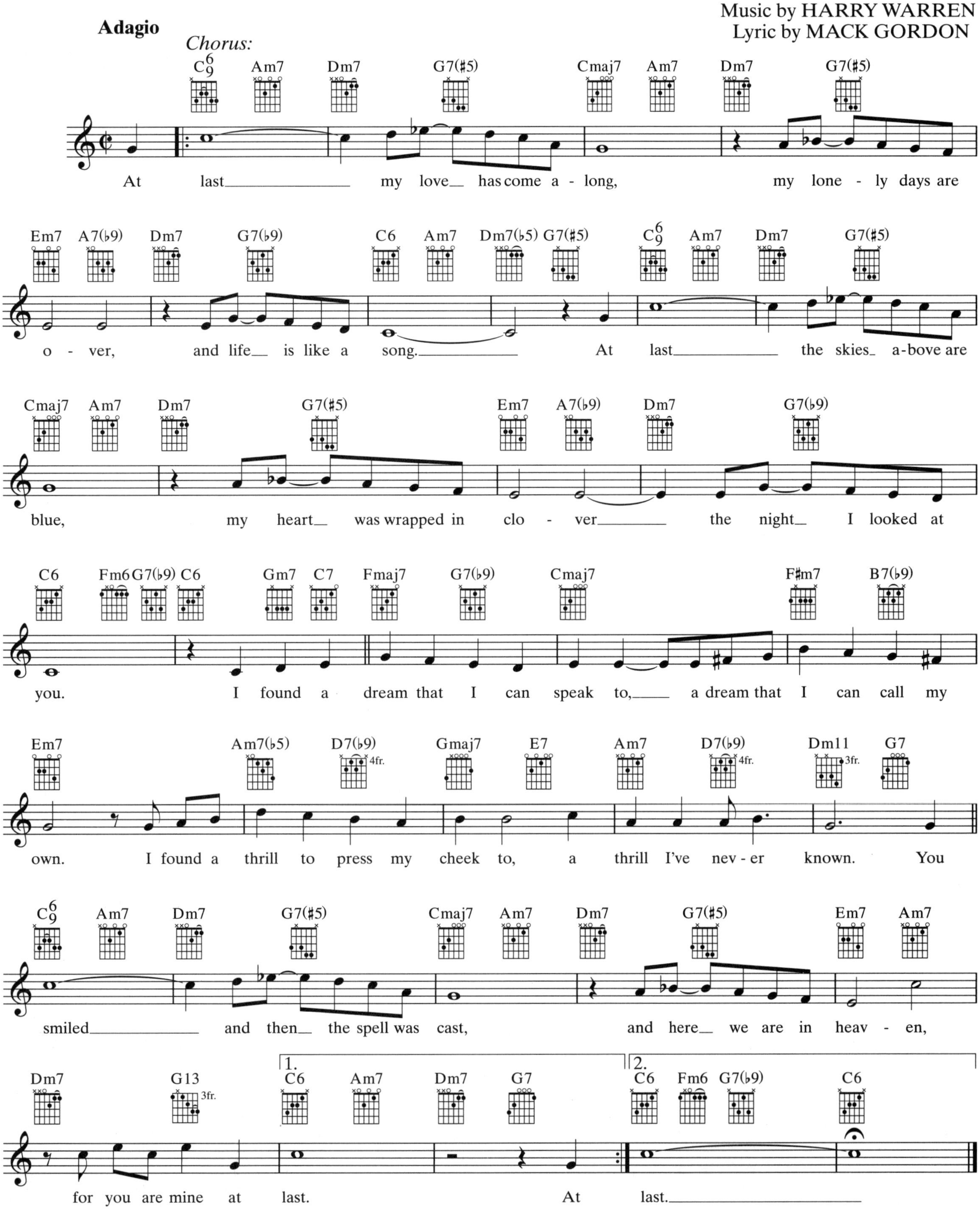

BEGIN THE BEGUINE

Music and Lyrics by
COLE PORTER

Medium swing or Beguine

When they be-gin the be-guine it brings back the sound of mu-sic so ten-der, it brings back a night of trop-i-cal splen-dour, it brings back a mem-o-ry ev-er green. I'm with you once more un-der the stars and down by the shore an or-ches-tra's play-ing, and e-ven the palms seem to be sway-ing when they be-gin the be-guine. To live it a-gain is past all en-deav-our, ex-cept when that tune clutch-es my heart, and there we are, swear-ing to love for-ev-er, and prom-is-ing nev-er, nev-er to part. What

Begin the Beguine - 2 - 1
27526

© 1935 WARNER BROS. INC. (Renewed)
All Rights Reserved

C C6 Cmaj7 C6 C
mo-ments di - vine, what rap-ture se - rene, till clouds came a - long to dis -
Em7(♭5) A7(♭9) Dm7 G7 Dm7(♭5)
perse the joys we had tast - ed and now when I hear peo-ple curse the chance that was
Fm6 Dm7 G13 Cmaj7 C6
wast - ed, I know but too well what they mean; so don't
C C6 Cmaj7 C6 C
let them be - gin the be - guine. Let the love that was once a -
C6 G7 Fmaj7 Dm7
fire re-main an em - ber. Let it sleep like the dead de - sire I on - ly re -
Em7 A7(♭9) Dm7 G13 3fr. Cmaj7 Dm11 3fr. G11 3fr. G7(♭9)
mem - ber when they be - gin the be - guine. Oh yes,
C C6 Cmaj7 C6 C Dm7/C C Em7 E♭dim7
let them be-gin the be - guine, make them play till the stars that were there be - fore re - turn a -
G7/D G7 Fmaj7 Dm7 Em7 A7(♭9) Dm7
bove you, till you whis-per to me once more, 'Dar-ling, I love you!' and we sud-den-ly know
Dm7(♭5) Fm6 G11 G7 C Dm7 G7
what heav-en we're in, when they be - gin the be - guine.
LAST TIME
Dm7 G11 C C6 Cmaj7 C6 C
When they be - gin the be - guine.

THE BEST THINGS IN LIFE ARE FREE

Music and Lyrics by
B.G. DESYLVA, LEW BROWN
and RAY HENDERSON

Medium/bright

The moon be-longs to ev-'ry-one, the best things in life are free. The stars be-long to ev-'ry-one, they gleam there for you and me. The flow-ers in spring, the rob-ins that sing, the sun-beams that shine: they're yours, they're mine! And love can come to ev-'ry-one, the best things in life are free. The free.

© 1948 (Renewed) CHAPPELL & CO., STEPHEN BALLENTINE MUSIC
and RAY HENDERSON MUSIC in the U.S.A.
All Rights Reserved

BEWITCHED

Words by LORENZ HART
Music by RICHARD RODGERS

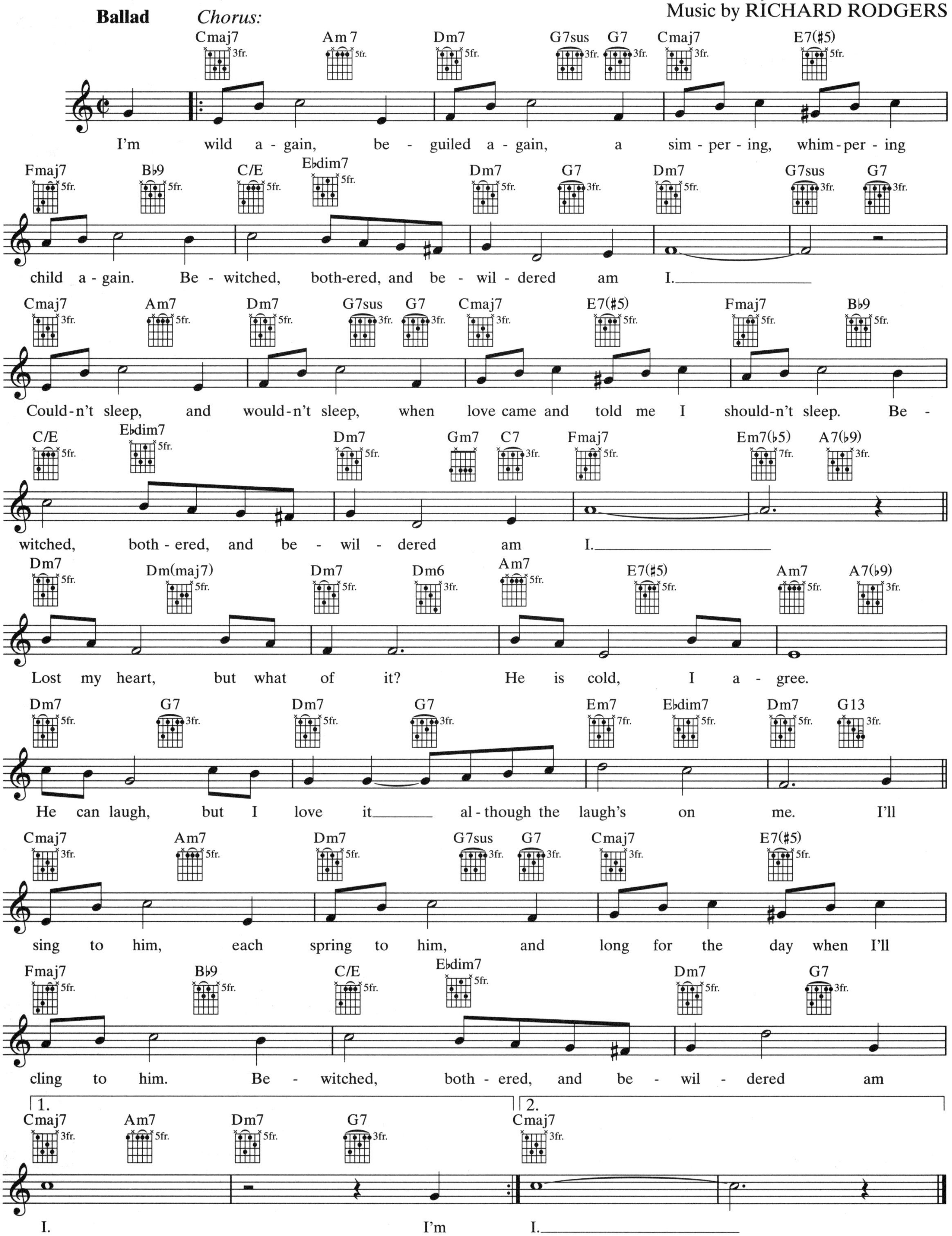

BLUE MOON

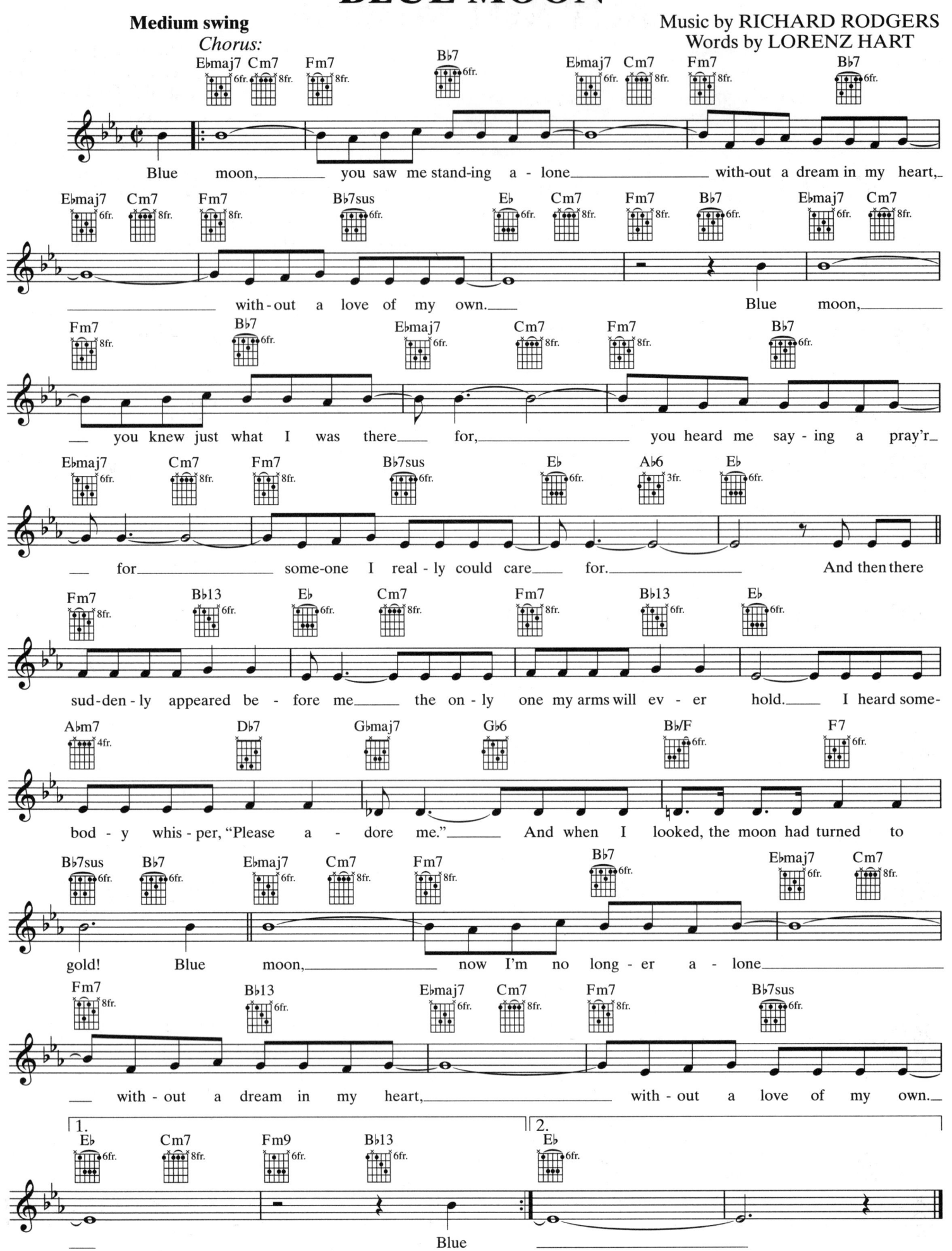

Medium swing

Chorus:

Music by RICHARD RODGERS
Words by LORENZ HART

Blue moon, you saw me standing a-lone with-out a dream in my heart, with-out a love of my own. Blue moon, you knew just what I was there for, you heard me say-ing a pray'r for some-one I real-ly could care for. And then there sud-den-ly appeared be-fore me the on-ly one my arms will ev-er hold. I heard some-bod-y whis-per, "Please a-dore me." And when I looked, the moon had turned to gold! Blue moon, now I'm no long-er a-lone with-out a dream in my heart, with-out a love of my own.

1.
2. Blue

© 1934 (Renewed 1962) METRO-GOLDWYN-MAYER INC.
All Rights Controlled by EMI ROBBINS CATALOG INC. (Publishing and ALFRED PUBLISHING CO., INC. (Print)
All Rights Reserved

BUT NOT FOR ME

Music and Lyrics by
GEORGE GERSHWIN
and IRA GERSHWIN

Ballad or Medium Swing *Chorus:*

They're writ-ing songs of love, but not for me.
on a door, but not for me.

A luck-y star's a-bove, but not for me.
He'll plan a two by four, but not for me.

With love to lead the way, I've found more clouds of gray
I know that love's a game; I'm puz-zled, just the same,

than an-y Rus-sian play could guar-an-tee. I was a
was I the moth or flame? I'm all at sea. It all be-

fool to fall and get that way; Heigh - ho! A-
gan so well, but what an end! This is the

las! and al - so, Lack - a - day! Al - though I
time a fell - er needs a friend, when ev - 'ry

can't dis - miss the mem - 'ry of his kiss, I guess he's
hap - py plot ends with the mar - riage knot, and there's no

|1. |2.|
not for me. He's knock-ing me.
knot for

© 1930 WB MUSIC CORP. (Renewed)
All Rights Reserved

COME FLY WITH ME

Lyric by SAMMY CAHN
Music by JAMES VAN HEUSEN

Med. swing

Chorus:

Come fly with me! Let's fly, let's fly a-way. If you can use some ex-ot-ic booze, there's a bar in far Bom-bay, come fly with me. Let's fly, let's fly a-way.

Come fly with me! Let's float down to Pe-ru! In Lla-ma Land there's a one-man band and he'll toot his flute for you, come fly with me. Let's take off in the blue!

(Once I get you) Up there, where the air is rar-i-fied,

© 1958 by MARAVILLE MUSIC CORP.
© Renewed and Assigned to MARAVILLE MUSIC CORP. and CAHN MUSIC CO.
All Rights on behalf of CAHN MUSIC CO. Administered by WB MUSIC CORP.
All Rights Reserved

B♭m7 E♭7 A♭6 B♭m7 E♭11
we'll just glide, star - ry - eyed, once I get you
A♭maj7 A♭+ A♭6 Gmaj7 E7(♭9)
up there, I'll be hold - ing you so near,
Am11 D13 G7 G11 G7 B♭7/A♭ Dm7/A G7(♭9)
you may hear, an - gels cheer, 'cause we're to - geth - er.
Cmaj7 C6 Em7 E♭dim7
Weath - er - wise it's such a love - ly day!
Dm7 G7 Cmaj7 C6 Gm7 C13
Just say the words and we'll beat the birds down to
Fmaj7 B♭13 Cmaj7 C6 F9
A - ca - pul - co Bay. It's per - fect for a fly - ing hon - ey -
Em7(♭5) B♭9 A7(♭9) D9 Dm7 G7
moon, they say, come fly with me. Let's fly, let's fly a -
1. C Dm7 G7
way. Come
2. C
way!

DO NOTHIN' TIL YOU HEAR FROM ME

Music by DUKE ELLINGTON
Lyric by BOB RUSSELL

Slow / Med.

Do noth-in' till you hear from me, pay no at-ten-tion to what's said.

Why peo-ple tear the seam of an-y-one's dream is o-ver my head.

Do noth-in' till you hear from me, at least con-sid-er our ro-mance. If you should take the word of

oth-er's you've heard, I have-n't a chance. True, I've been

seen with some-one new, but does that mean that I'm un-true? When we're a-

part the words in my heart re-veal how I feel a-bout you. Some kiss may cloud my mem-o-

ry, and oth-er arms may hold a thrill. But please do noth-in' till you hear it from me,

1. and you nev-er will.
2. Do noth-in' till you hear from

© 1943 (Renewed) FAMOUS MUSIC CORPORATION and HARRISON MUSIC CORP. in the U.S.
All Rights Outside of the U.S. Controlled by EMI Robbins Catalog INC. (Publishing) and ALFRED PUBLISHING CO., INC. (Print)
All Rights Reserved

DON'T GET AROUND MUCH ANYMORE

Music by DUKE ELLINGTON
Lyric by BOB RUSSELL

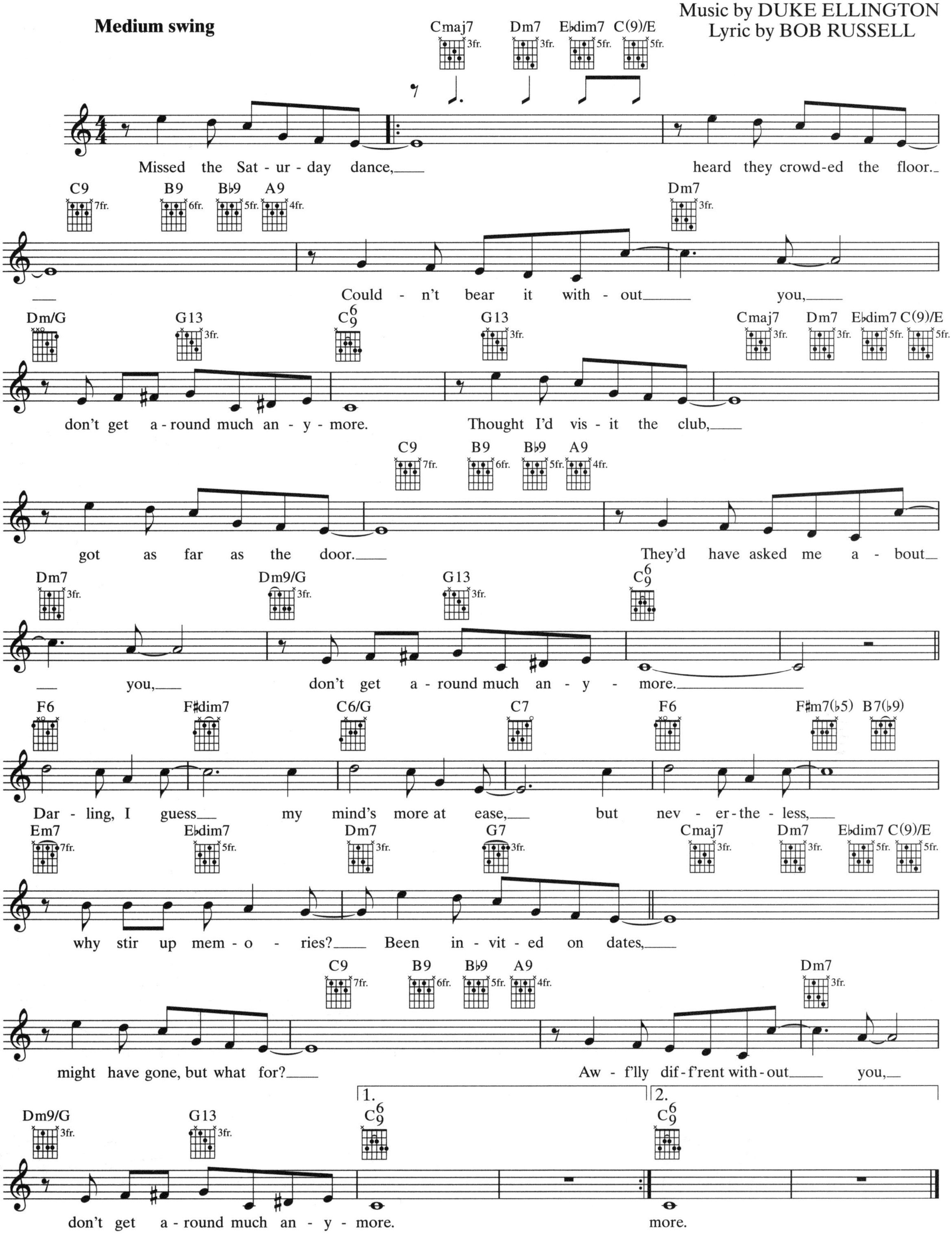

A FOGGY DAY

Music and Lyrics by
GEORGE GERSHWIN
and IRA GERSHWIN

Freely
Verse:

| F | Gm7/F | Fmaj7 | F7 | Gm7 | C9 |

I was a strang-er in the cit-y. Out of town were the peo-ple I knew.

| F | E7 | Am7 | D9 |

I had the feel-ing of self - pi - ty. What to do? What to do? What to do? The

| Gm7 | C7(♭9) | C7(♭9♯5) | Fmaj7 | F6 | Am7 | Am6 |

out - look was de - cid - ed - ly blue. But as I walked through the fog - gy

| Am7 | D13 | Am7 | Adim7 | Gm7 | C13 | F | Gm7/C | F | C7 |

streets a - lone, it turned out to be the luck - iest day I've known. A

Moderately
Chorus:

| Fmaj7 | Cm7(♭5) | Gm7 | C13 | C7(♭9) |

fog - gy day in Lon - don town

| F6 | Fm7/E♭ | Dm7(♭5) | G13 | G7(♯5) | C9 |

had me low, and had me down.

| Fmaj7 | F9 | B♭maj7 | B♭m6 |

I viewed the morn-ing with a - larm, the

Fmaj7 D9 G13 G9(♯5) C9
Brit - ish Mu - se - um had lost its charm. How
Fmaj7 Cm7(♭5) Gm7 C13 C13(♭9)
long, I won - dered, could this thing last? But the
F6 Fm7/E♭ Dm7(♭5) G13 G7(♯5) C9
age of mir - a - cles had - n't passed, for,
Fsus F13 F13(♭9) B♭maj7 Bm6(maj7)
sud - den - ly, I saw you there and through
F/A B♭6 Fmaj7/C B♭6 Dm7 G7
fog - gy Lon - don town the sun was shin - ing
Gm7/C C7
ev - 'ry - where.
1. F/A A♭13 Gm7 C9
A
2. F B♭13 B♭maj7 Fmaj7
8va
where.
3fr. 4fr. 5fr. 6fr. 8fr. 2fr.

I CAN'T GET STARTED

Words by IRA GERSHWIN
Music by VERNON DUKE

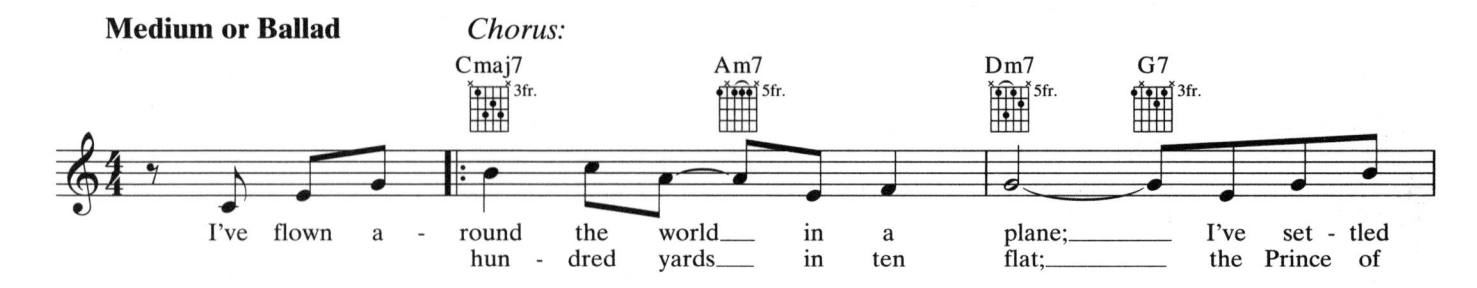

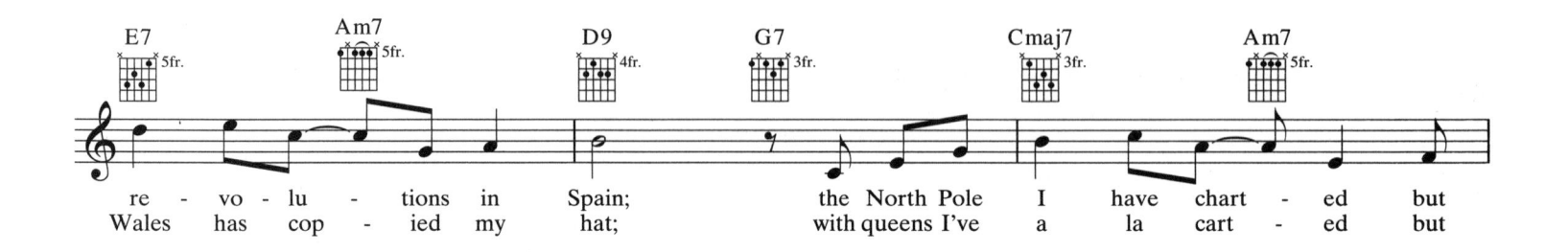

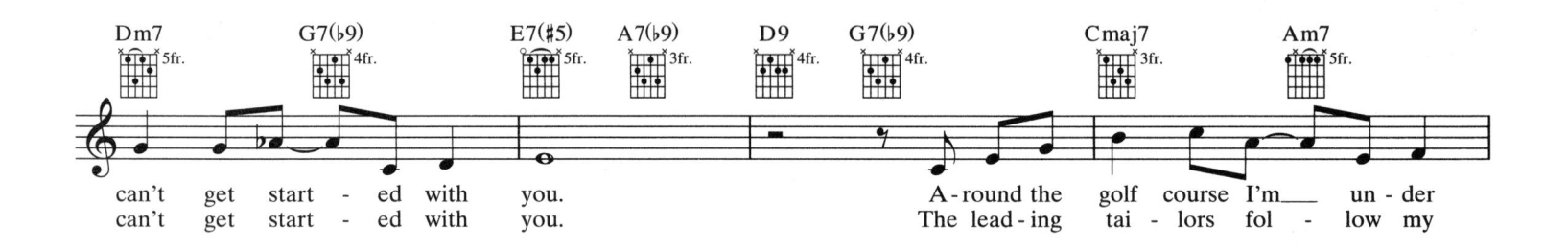

Medium or Ballad   *Chorus:*

I've flown a-round the world__ in a plane;_____ I've set-tled
hun-dred yards__ in ten flat;_____ the Prince of

re - vo - lu - tions in Spain; the North Pole I have chart - ed but
Wales has cop - ied my hat; with queens I've a la cart - ed but

can't get start - ed with you. A - round the golf course I'm__ un - der
can't get start - ed with you. The lead - ing tai - lors fol - low my

par,_____ and all the mov - ies want__ me to star; I've got a
styles,_____ and tooth-paste ads all fea - ture my smiles; the As - tor-

© 1935 (Renewed) IRA GERSHWIN MUSIC and CHAPPELL & CO., INC.
All Rights on behalf of IRA GERSHWIN MUSIC Administered by WB MUSIC CORP.
All Rights Reserved

Cmaj7 Am7 Dm7 G7(♭9) Cmaj7 Fm6 Cmaj7
house, a show - place, but I get no___ place with you. You're so su -
bilts I vis - it, but say what is___ it with you? When first we
Em11 A7 Em9 A13 Dmaj7 Dmaj9
preme, lyr - ics I write__ of you, scheme just for a sight__ of you,
met, how you e - lat - ed me, Pet, you dev - as - tat - ed me!
Dm7 G9 Dm9 G13 Em11 E♭dim7 Dm7 G7
dream both day and night__ of you, and what good does it do? In nine - teen
Yet, now you've de - flat - ed me till you're my Wa - ter - loo. I've sold my
Cmaj7 Am7 Dm7 G7 E7 Am7
twen - ty - nine___ I sold short;______ in En - gland I'm pre - sen - ted at
kiss - es at___ a ba - zaar,______ and af - ter me they've named_ a ci -
D9 G7 Cmaj7 A7(♭9 ♯5) Dm9 G7
court, but you've got me down - heart - ed 'cause I can't get start - ed with
gar; but late - ly how I've smart - ed 'cause I can't get start - ed with
1. C6/9 A7(♯5) Dm7 G7 2. C6/9
you. I do a you.______________

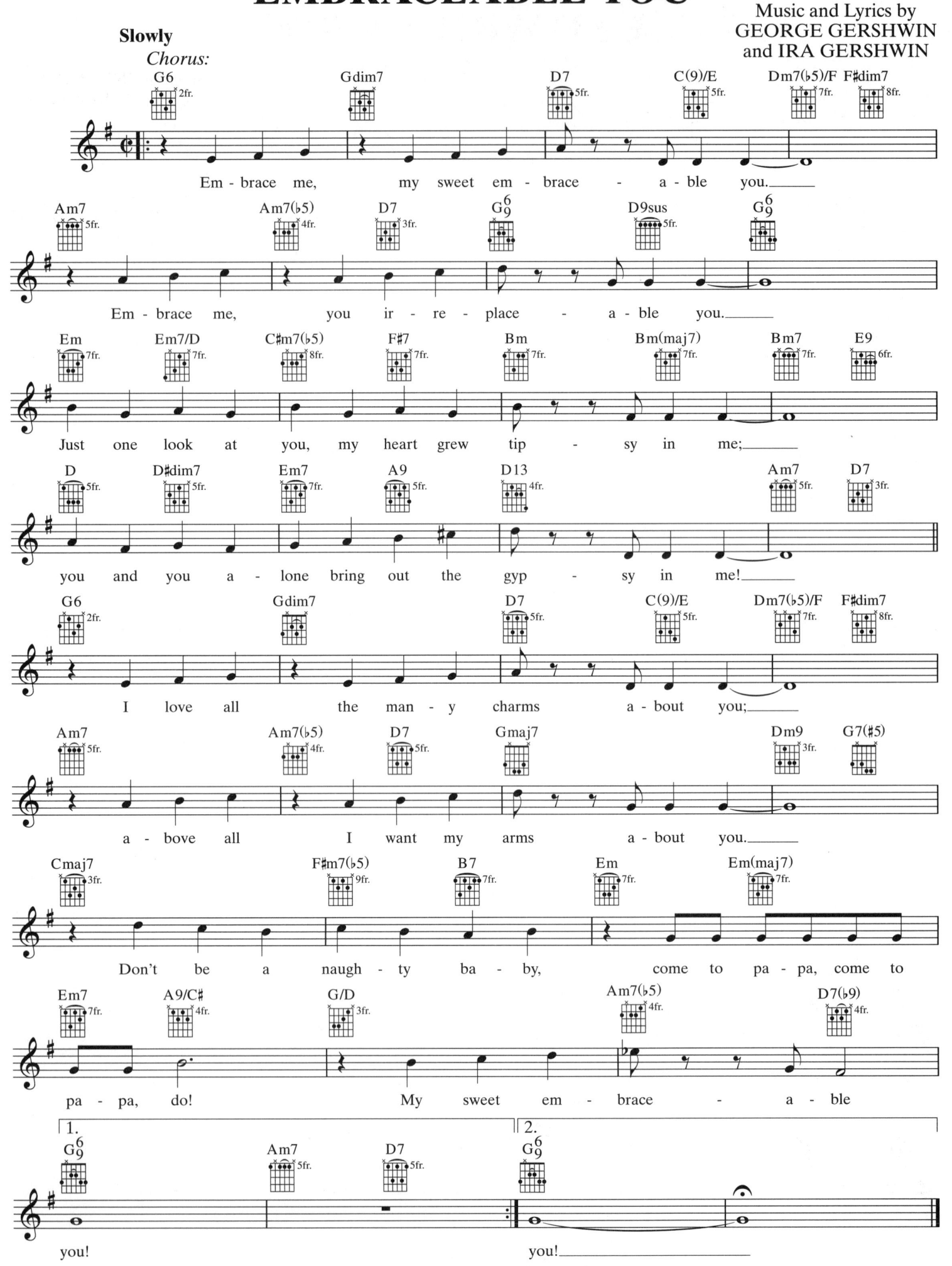

EMBRACEABLE YOU

Music and Lyrics by
GEORGE GERSHWIN
and IRA GERSHWIN

Slowly
Chorus:

Em - brace me, my sweet em - brace - a - ble you.

Em - brace me, you ir - re - place - a - ble you.

Just one look at you, my heart grew tip - sy in me;

you and you a - lone bring out the gyp - sy in me!

I love all the man - y charms a - bout you;

a - bove all I want my arms a - bout you.

Don't be a naugh - ty ba - by, come to pa - pa, come to

pa - pa, do! My sweet em - brace - a - ble

1. you!

2. you!

© 1930 WB MUSIC CORP. (Renewed)
All Rights Reserved

I COULD WRITE A BOOK

Words by LORENZ HART
Music by RICHARD RODGERS

Medium *Chorus:*

If they asked me I could write a book, a-bout the way you walk and whis-per and look. I could write a pre-face on how we met, so the world would nev-er for-get. And the sim-ple se-cret of the plot is just to tell them that I love you a lot. Then the world dis-cov-ers as my book ends, how to make two

1. lov-ers of friends.
2. If they friends.

© 1940 (Renewed) CHAPPELL & CO.
Rights for Extended Renewal Term in the U.S. Administered by WB MUSIC CORP. and WILLIAMSON MUSIC
All Rights Reserved

I GET A KICK OUT OF YOU

Music and Lyrics by
COLE PORTER

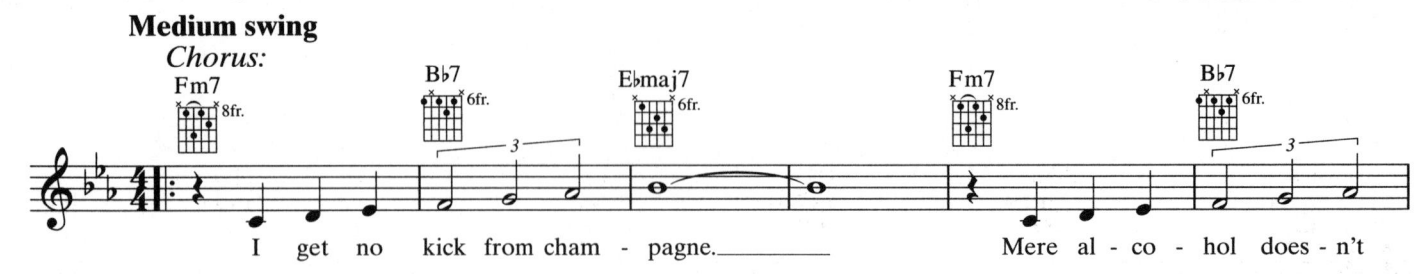

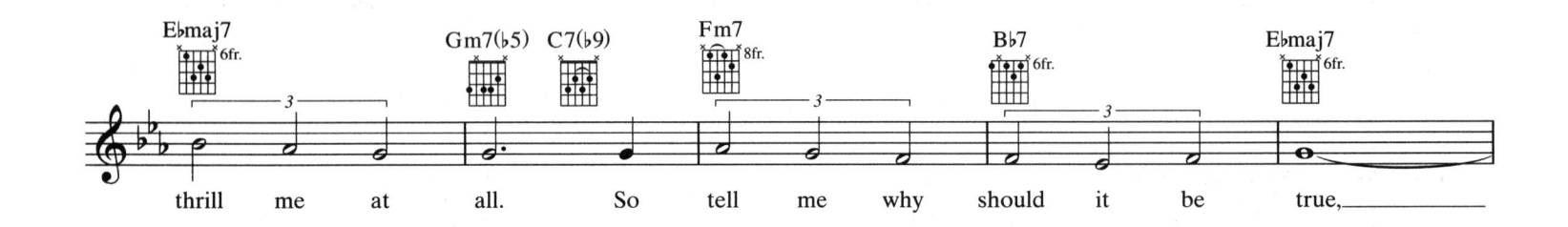

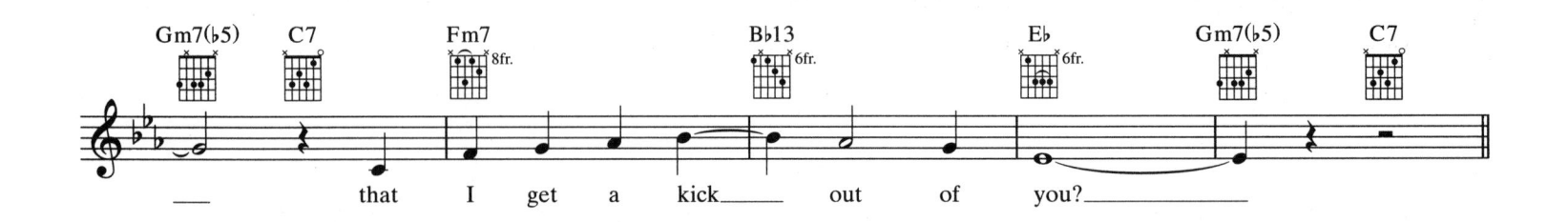

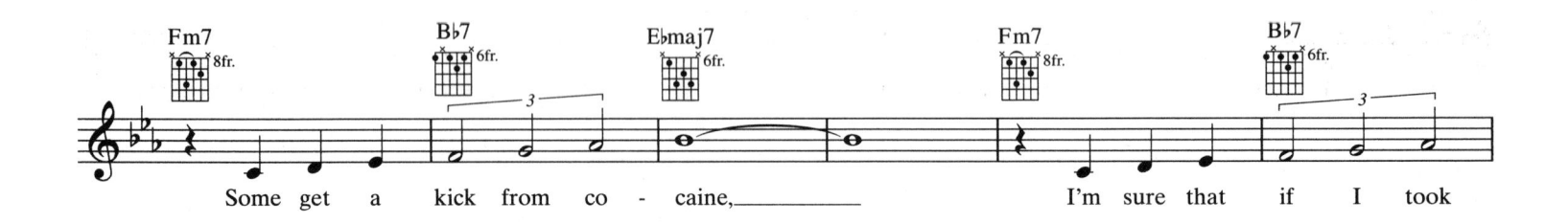

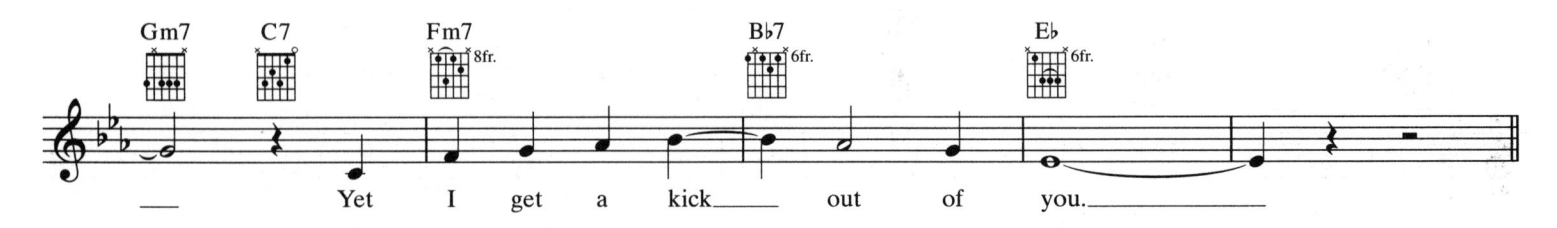

Medium swing
Chorus:

I get no kick from cham - pagne. Mere al - co - hol does - n't thrill me at all. So tell me why should it be true, that I get a kick out of you?

Some get a kick from co - caine, I'm sure that if I took e - ven one sniff that would bore me ter - rif - ic - 'lly too. Yet I get a kick out of you.

I Get a Kick out of You - 2 - 1
27526

© 1934 WARNER BROS. INC. (Renewed)
All Rights Reserved

E♭7 A♭/E♭ E♭7 D♭/A♭ A♭ D♭/A♭ A♭ E♭6 E♭7
I get a kick ev - 'ry time I see you stand - ing
E♭6 Edim7 C7 Fm7 B♭7
there be - fore me. I get a kick tho' it's
Gm7(♭5)/F Fm7 Gm7(♭5)/F Fm7 F9 B♭7sus B♭7
clear to me you ob - vious - ly don't a - dore me.
Fm7 B♭7 E♭maj7 Fm7 B♭7
I get no kick in a plane. Fly - ing too high with some
E♭ G7 Cm7 Fm7 B♭7 C7
(gal) in the sky is my i - dea of noth - ing to do. Yet
(guy)
Fm7 B♭7 1. E♭ Gm7(♭5) C7 2. E♭ B♭7sus E♭
I get a kick out of you. you

I ONLY HAVE EYES FOR YOU

Words by AL DUBIN
Music by HARRY WARREN

Freely
Verse:

My love must be a kind of blind love, I can't see any-one but you. And, dear, I won-der if you find love an op-ti-cal il-lu-sion too? Are the

Slow / Med.
Chorus:

stars out to-night? I don't know if it's cloud-y or bright. 'Cause I on-ly have eyes for you, dear. The moon may be high, but I can't see a thing in the sky. 'Cause I

I Only Have Eyes for You - 2 - 1
27526

© 1934 WARNER BROS. INC. (Renewed)
All Rights Reserved

Cmaj7 E7(♭9 ♯5) A7
on - ly have eyes for you.
Dm7 G7sus G7 Em7 E♭9
I don't know if we're in a gar - den,
Dm7(♭5) G7 Em7 E♭m7 A♭13
or on a crowd - ed av - e - nue. You are
Dm11 A7(♯5) Dm7 G7 Dm7 G7
here, so am I. May - be mil - lions of peo - ple go
Dm7 G7 Cmaj7 F9(♯11) F9 B♭7(♯11)
by. But they all dis - ap - pear from view.
A7sus A7(♭9 ♯5) Dm7 Fm6/G G7(♭9)
And I on - ly have eyes for
1. C Dm7 G7(♭9) 2. C G7sus C
you. Are the you.

I GOT RHYTHM

Music and Lyrics by
GEORGE GERSHWIN
and IRA GERSHWIN

Lively

Chorus:

I got rhythm, I got music,

I got my man, who could ask for anything more?

I got daisies in green pastures,

I got my man, who could ask for anything more?

Old Man Trouble, I don't mind him,

you won't find him 'round my door.

I got starlight, I got sweet dreams,

1. I got my man, who could ask for anything more?

2. ask for anything more? Who could ask for anything more?

© 1930 WB MUSIC CORP. (Renewed)
All Rights Reserved

I WANNA BE AROUND

Words and Music by
JOHNNY MERCER and
SADIE VIMMERSTEDT

I'LL BE SEEING YOU

Words and Music by
SAMMY FAIN and IRVING KAHAL

Slowly

I'll be seeing you__ in all the old fa-mil-iar plac-es that this heart of mine em-brac-es all day thru:__ In that small ca-fé,__ the park a-cross the way,__ the chil-dren's ca-rou-sel,__ the chest-nut trees,__ the wish-ing well.__ I'll be see-ing you__ in ev-'ry love-ly sum-mer's day, in ev-'ry-thing that's light and gay, I'll al-ways think of you that way. I'll find you in the morn-ing sun and when the night is new. I'll be look-ing at the moon,__ but I'll be see-ing you!

© 1938 (Renewed) WILLIAMSON MUSIC, INC.
Rights for the Extended Renewal Term in the U.S. Assigned to
FRED AHLERT MUSIC CORPORATION, THE NEW IRVING KAHAL MUSIC COMPANY and FAIN MUSIC COMPANY
All Rights for FRED AHLERT MUSIC CORPORATION and TED KOEHLER MUSIC Administered by BUG MUSIC, INC.
All Rights Reserved   Used by Permission

I'LL SEE YOU IN MY DREAMS

Words by GUS KAHN
Music by ISHAM JONES

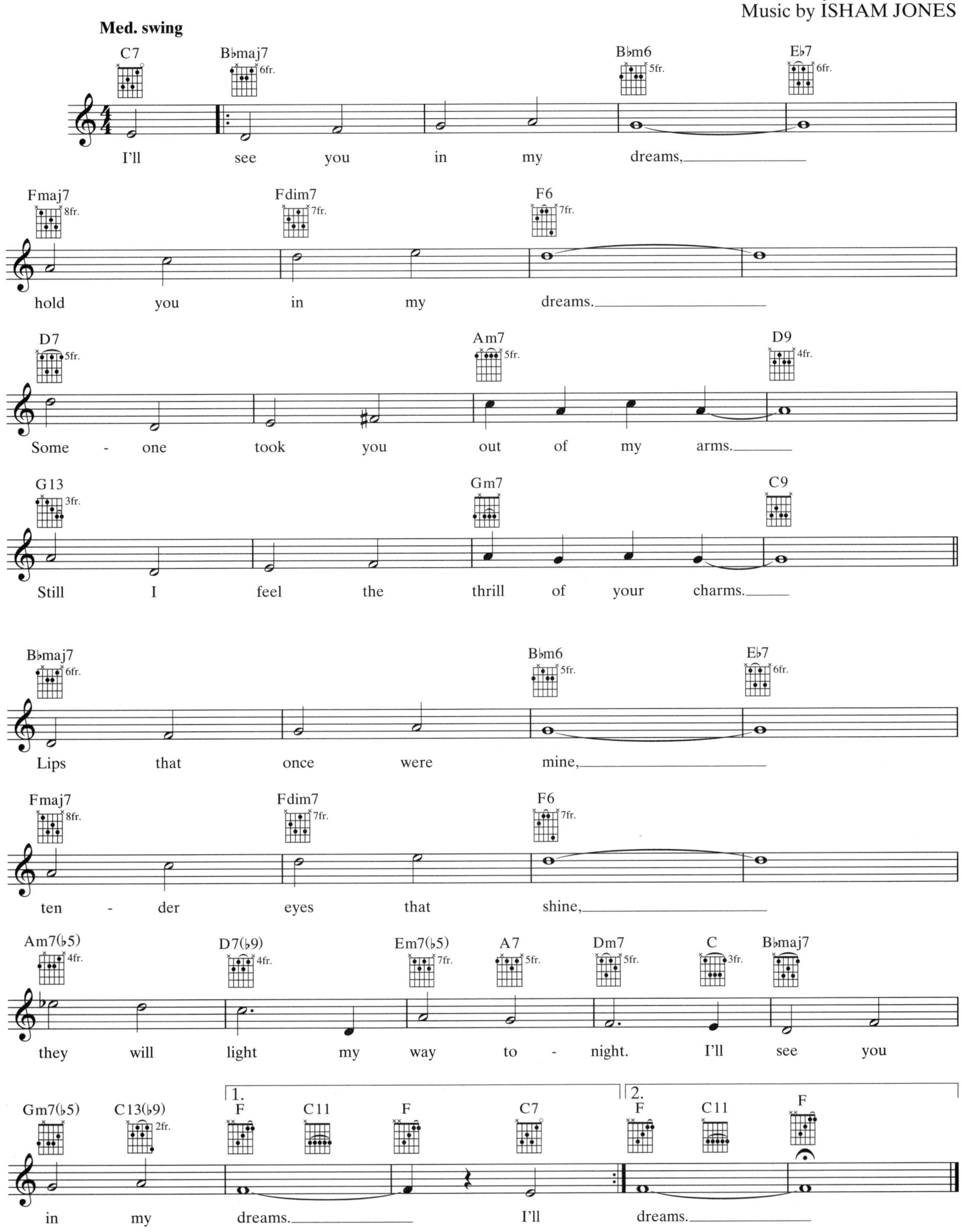

I'M IN THE MOOD FOR LOVE

Words and Music by
JIMMY McHUGH
and DOROTHY FIELDS

Med./ballad

I'VE GOT A CRUSH ON YOU

Music and Lyrics by
GEORGE GERSHWIN
and IRA GERSHWIN

Moderate   *Chorus:*

I've got a crush on you, Sweetie Pie.
crush on you, Sweetie Pie.

All the day and night-time hear me sigh. I never had the least
All the day and night-time hear me sigh. This isn't just a flir-

no - tion that I could fall with so much e - mo - tion.
ta - tion: we're prov - ing that there's pre - des - ti - na - tion.

Could you coo, could you care for a cun - ning cot - tage
I could coo, I could care for that cun - ning cot - tage

we could share? The world will par - don my mush, 'cause I've got a
we could share. Your mush I nev - er shall shush, 'cause I've got a

crush, my ba - by, on you. I've got a you.
crush, my ba - by, on

© 1930 WB MUSIC CORP. (Renewed)
All Rights Reserved

I'VE GOT YOU UNDER MY SKIN

Music and Lyrics by
COLE PORTER

Medium

I've got you under my skin. I've got you deep in the heart of me. So deep in my heart, you're really a part of me. I've got you under my skin. I tried so not to give in. I said to myself, "This affair never will go so well." But why should I try to resist when, darling, I know so well, I've

I've Got You Under My Skin - 2 - 1
27526

© 1936 CHAPPELL & CO. (Renewed)
All Rights Reserved

Fm7 8fr. Bb11 6fr. Ebmaj7 6fr. Eb6 5fr.
got you under my skin. I'd
Fm7/Eb 5fr. Bb7/Eb 6fr. Ebmaj7 6fr. Eb7 6fr.
sac - ri - fice an - y - thing, come what might, for the sake of hav - ing you near. In spite of a
Fm7/Eb 5fr. Fm7(b5)/Eb 4fr. Gm7 5fr. Gb7 4fr. Fm11 6fr. Bb7 6fr.
warn - ing voice that comes in the night and re - peats and re - peats in my ear: "Don't you
Cm7 3fr. Fm7 8fr. Bb7(#5) 6fr. Ebmaj7 6fr. Gm7 Gbdim7
know, lit - tle fool, you nev - er can win. Use your men -
Fm11 6fr. Bb13 6fr. Ebmaj7 6fr.
tal - i - ty. Wake up to re - al - i - ty."
Bbm7 6fr. Eb7(b9) 5fr. Ab6 3fr. Abm6 3fr.
But each time I do, just the thought of you makes me
Eb6 5fr. Gm7(b5) C7(b9) Fm9 Bb13 6fr.
stop be - fore I be - gin, 'cause I've got you un - der my
1. Eb 6fr. Gm7 C7(b9)
skin. I've
2. Eb 6fr. Bb11 6fr. Eb 6fr.
skin.

I'VE GROWN ACCUSTOMED TO HER FACE

Lyrics by ALAN J. LERNER
Music by FREDERICK LOEWE

Slow

I've grown ac - cus - tomed to her face. _____ She al - most
cus - tomed to her face. _____ She al - most

makes the day be - gin. _____ I've grown ac - cus - tomed to the tune she
makes the day be - gin. _____ I've got - ten used to hear her say: "Good

whis - tles night and noon, her smiles, her frowns, her ups, her downs are sec - ond
morn - ing" ev - 'ry day, her joys, her woes, her highs, her lows are sec - ond

na - ture to me now; _____ like breath - ing out and breath - ing in. _____
na - ture to me now; _____ like breath - ing out and breath - ing in. _____

___ I was se - rene - ly in - de - pen - dent and con - tent be - fore we met;
___ I'm ver - y grate - ful she's a wom - an and so eas - y to for - get;

sure - ly I could al - ways be that way a - gain and yet, I've grown ac - cus - tomed to her looks; ac -
rath - er like a ha - bit one can al - ways break and yet, I've grown ac - cus - tomed to the trace of

cus - tomed to her voice; ac - cus - tomed to her face. I've grown ac - face.
some - thing in the air; ac - cus - tomed to her

© 1956 Alan J. Lerner and Frederick Loewe
Copyright Renewed
Chappell & Co., owner of publication and allied rights throughout the World
All Rights Reserved

IT HAD TO BE YOU

Words by GUS KAHN
Music by ISHAM JONES

Freely

Chorus:

It had to be you, it had to be you. I wan-dered a-round and fi-nal-ly found the some-bod-y who could make me be true, could make me be blue and e-ven be glad, just to be sad, think-ing of you. Some oth-ers I've seen might nev-er be mean. Might nev-er be cross, or try to be boss, but they would-n't do. For no-bod-y else gave me a thrill. With all your faults, I love you still. It had to be you, won-der-ful you, had to be you. It had to be you,

© 1924 (Renewed) WARNER BROS. INC.
All Rights for the Extended Term in the U.S. Controlled by
THE BANTAM MUSIC PUBLISHING CO. and GILBERT KEYES MUSIC COMPANY
All Rights Administered by WB MUSIC CORP.
All Rights Reserved

THE LADY IS A TRAMP

In strict tempo

Words by LORENZ HART
Music by RICHARD RODGERS

Verse:

I've wined and dined on mul-li-gan stew and nev-er wished for tur-key, as I hitched and hiked and grift-ed, too,* from Maine to Al-bu-quer-que. A-las, I missed the Beaux-Arts Ball, and what is twice as sad, I was nev-er at a par-ty where they hon-ored No-el Ca-'ad. But so-cial cir-cles spin too fast for me, my Ho-bo-hem-ia is the place to be.

Chorus:

I get too hun-gry for din-ner at eight. I like the thea-ter, but nev-er come late. I nev-er both-er with peo-ple I hate. That's why the la-dy is a tramp.

I go to Co-net, the beach is di-vine. I go to ball games, the bleach-ers are fine. I fol-low Winch-ell and read ev-'ry line. That's why the la-dy is a tramp.

*Alternative version: and drifted, too

The Lady Is a Tramp - 2 - 1
27526

© 1937 (Renewed) CHAPPELL & CO.
Rights for Extended Renewal Term in the U.S. Administered by WB MUSIC CORP. and WILLIAMSON MUSIC
All Rights Reserved

Refrain 3 (reprise):
Don't know the reason for cocktails at five.
I don't like flying – I'm glad I'm alive.
I crave affection, but not when I drive.
That's why the lady is a tramp.
Folks go to London and leave me behind,
I'll miss the crowning, Queen Mary won't mind.
I don't play Scarlett in Gone With The Wind.
That's why the lady is a tramp.
I like to hang my hat where I please,
Sail with the breeze.
No dough – heigh-ho!
I love La Guardia and think he's a champ.
That's why the lady is a tramp.

Refrain 4 (reprise):
Girls get massages, they cry and they moan.
Tell Lizzie Arden to leave me alone.
I'm not so hot, but my shape is my own.
That's why the lady is a tramp.
The food at Sardi's is perfect, no doubt.
I wouldn't know what the Ritz's is about.
I drop a nickel and coffee comes out.
That's why the lady is a tramp!
I like the sweet, fresh rain in my face,
Diamonds and lace,
No got – so what?
For Robert Taylor I whistle and stamp.
That's why the lady is a tramp!

LET'S DO IT
(Let's Fall in Love)

Music and Lyrics by
COLE PORTER

Freely *Verse:*

When the lit-tle blue-bird, who has nev-er said a word, starts to sing: "Spring, spring"; when the lit-tle blue-bell, in the bot-tom of the dell, starts to ring: "Ding, ding"; when the lit-tle blue clerk, in the mid-dle of his work, starts a tune to the moon up a-bove, it is na-ture, that's all, sim-ply tell-ing us to fall in love. And that's why

Medium *Chorus:*

birds do it, bees do it, e-ven ed-u-ca-ted fleas do it,
spon-ges, they say, do it, oy-sters down in Oy-ster Bay do it,

Let's Do It - 2 - 1
27526

© 1928 WARNER BROS. INC. (Renewed)
All Rights Reserved

B♭6 G7 Cm7 F7 B♭maj7 Gm7 Cm7 F7
let's do it, let's fall in love. In Spain the
let's do it, let's fall in love. Cold Cape Cod
B♭6 Cm7 F7 B♭6 B♭7 E♭6 E♭m7
best up - per sets do it, Lith - u - a - ni - ans and Letts do it,
clams, 'gainst their wish, do it, e - ven la - zy jel - ly - fish do it,
B♭6 G7 Cm7 F7 B♭maj7 D7(♯5)
let's do it, let's fall in love. The Dutch in
let's do it, let's fall in love. E - lec - tric
Gm7 E♭7 Dm7 Fm7 B♭7
old Am - ster - dam do it, not to men - tion the Finns.
eels, I might add, do it, though it shocks 'em I know.
E♭maj7 A♭7 D♭maj7 Cm11 F7
Folks in Si - am do it, think of Si - am - ese twins. Some Ar - gen -
Why ask if shad do it, wait - er, bring me shad roe. In shal - low
B♭6 Cm7 F7 B♭6 B♭7 E♭7
tines with - out means do it, peo - ple say, in Bos - ton, e - ven beans do it,
shoals, Eng - lish soles do it, gold - fish in the pri - va - cy of bowls do it,
B♭6 Gm7 Cm7 F13 B♭maj7
1. Cm7 F7
2. B♭6
let's do it, let's fall in love. Ro - man - tic
let's do it, let's fall in love.
6fr.
3fr.
8fr.
5fr.
4fr.

LOVE FOR SALE

Words and Music by
COLE PORTER

Rubato

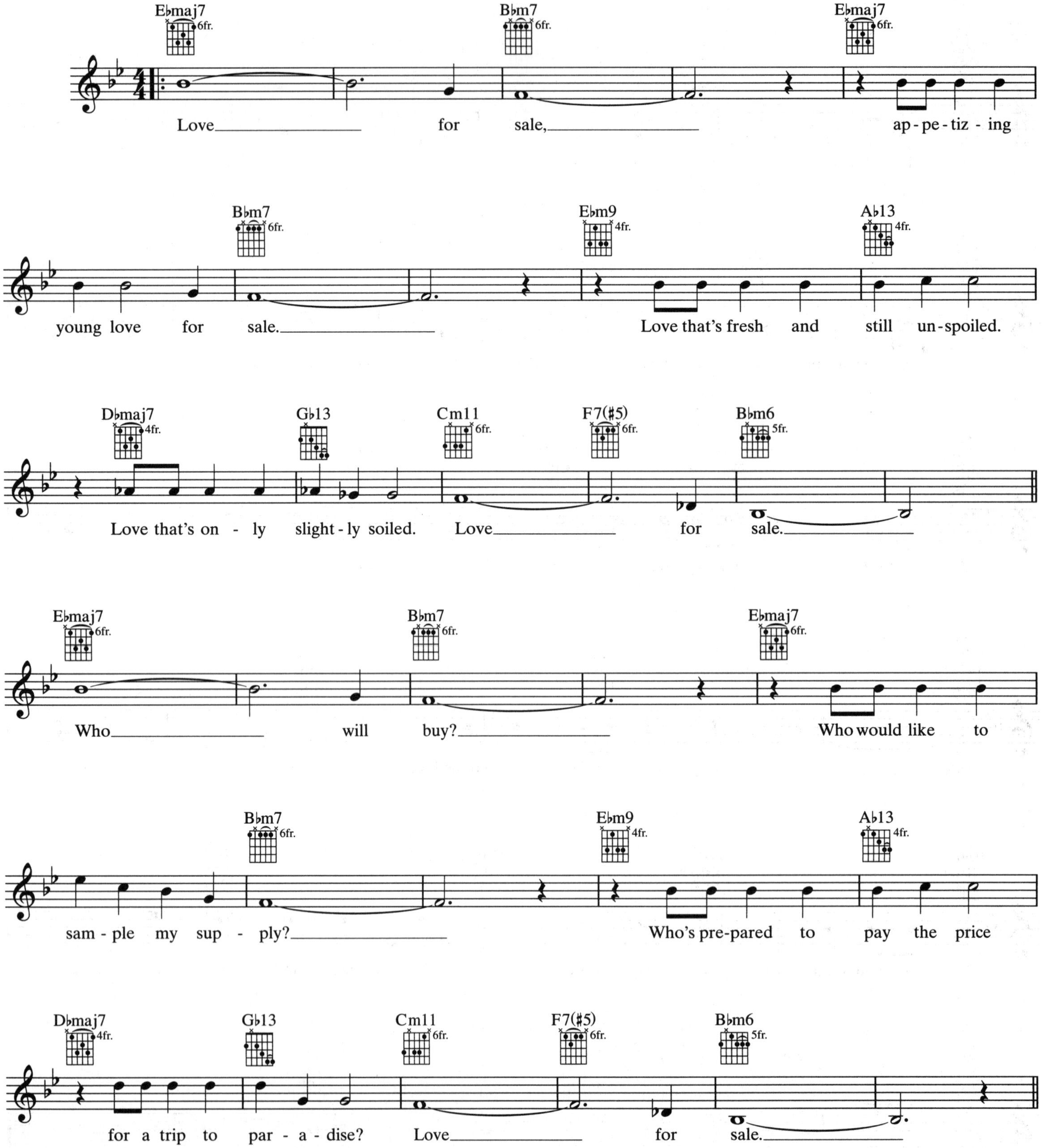

E♭m7 6fr.
A♭7(♭9)
D♭maj9 3fr.
Fm7 8fr.
B♭7(♭9) 4fr.
Let the po - ets pipe of love in their child - ish way.
E♭m7 6fr.
A♭7(♭9)
D♭maj7 4fr.
I know ev - 'ry type of love bet - ter far than they.
B♭7 6fr.
B7 7fr.
B♭7(♭9) 4fr.
E♭m7 6fr.
Gm7(♭5)
3
If you want the thrill of love I've been thru the mill of love; old love,
C7(♭9 ♯5)
Fm7(♭5)
B♭7(♭9)
E♭maj7 6fr.
new love. Ev - 'ry love but true love. Love for
B♭m7 6fr.
E♭maj7 6fr.
B♭m7 6fr.
sale. Ap - pe - tiz - ing young love for sale.
E♭m9 4fr.
A♭13 4fr.
D♭maj7 4fr.
G♭13
If you want to buy my wares, fol - low me and climb the stairs.
1.
2.
Cm11 6fr.
F7(♯5) 6fr.
B♭m6 5fr.
B♭7 6fr.
B♭m6 5fr.
Love for sale. sale.

LAURA

Lyrics by JOHNNY MERCER
Music by DAVID RAKSIN

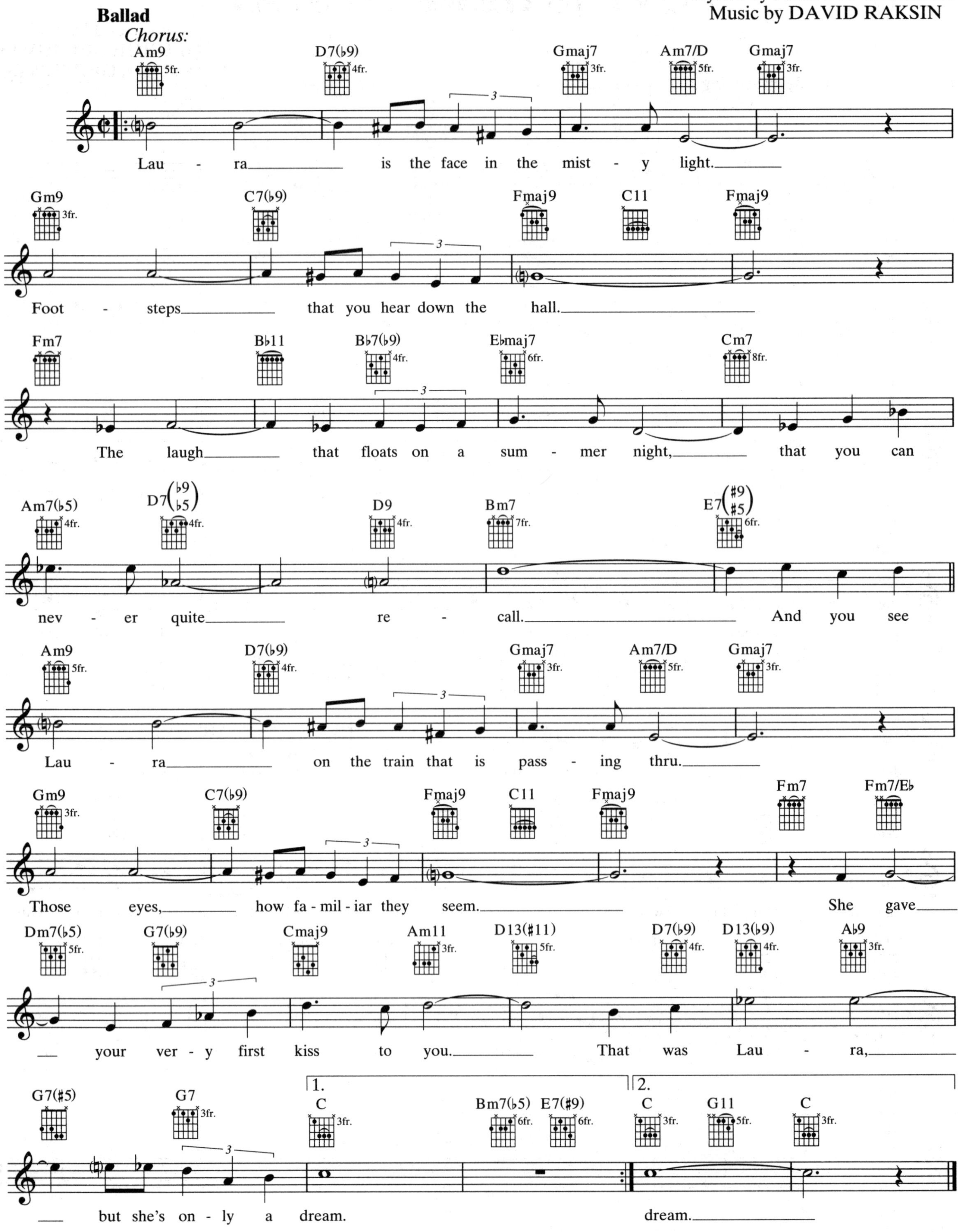

LOVE IS HERE TO STAY

Music and Lyrics by
GEORGE GERSHWIN
and IRA GERSHWIN

Moderate swing   *Chorus:*

It's ver-y clear our love is here to stay; not for a year but ev-er and a day. The ra-di-o and the tel-e-phone and the mov-ies that we know may just be pass-ing fan-cies, and in time may go. But, oh my dear, our love is here to stay; to-geth-er we're go-ing a long, long way. In time the Rock-ies may crum-ble, Gib-ral-tar may tum-ble, they're on-ly made of clay, but our love is

1. here to stay.____ It's ver-y
2. stay.____

© 1938 (Renewed 1965) GEORGE GERSHWIN MUSIC and IRA GERSHWIN MUSIC
All Rights Administered by WB MUSIC CORP.
All Rights Reserved

MOONGLOW

Words and Music by
WILL HUDSON, EDDIE DELANGE
and IRVING MILLS

I'LL SEE YOU IN MY DREAMS

Words by GUS KAHN
Music by ISHAM JONES

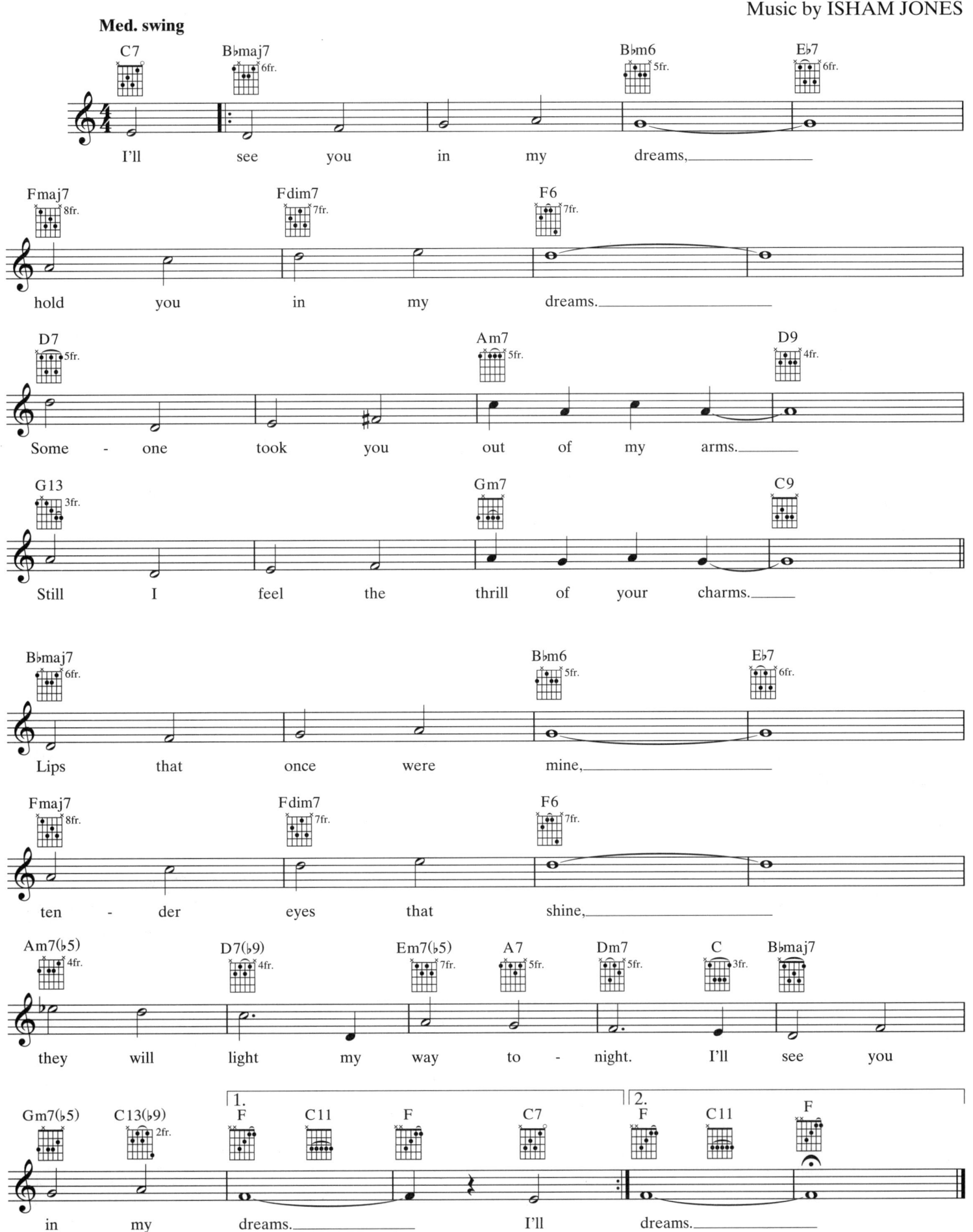

Med. swing

| C7 | B♭maj7 | | B♭m6 | E♭7 |

I'll see you in my dreams,____

| Fmaj7 | Fdim7 | F6 | |

hold you in my dreams.____

| D7 | | Am7 | D9 |

Some - one took you out of my arms.____

| G13 | | Gm7 | C9 |

Still I feel the thrill of your charms.____

| B♭maj7 | | B♭m6 | E♭7 |

Lips that once were mine,____

| Fmaj7 | Fdim7 | F6 | |

ten - der eyes that shine,____

| Am7(♭5) | D7(♭9) | Em7(♭5) | A7 | Dm7 | C | B♭maj7 |

they will light my way to - night. I'll see you

| Gm7(♭5) | C13(♭9) | **1.** F | C11 | F | C7 | **2.** F | C11 | F |

in my dreams.____ I'll dreams.____

© 1924 (Renewed) GILBERT KEYES MUSIC COMPANY and BANTAM MUSIC PUBLISHING CO.
All Rights in the U.S. Administered by WB MUSIC CORP.
All Rights Reserved

I'M IN THE MOOD FOR LOVE

Words and Music by
JIMMY McHUGH
and DOROTHY FIELDS

Med./ballad

I'm in the mood for love, sim-ply be-cause you're near me.
Fun-ny, but when you're near me, I'm in the mood for love.
Heav-en is in your eyes, bright as the stars we're un-der. Oh! Is it an-y
won-der? I'm in the mood for love. Why stop to think of wheth-er this lit-tle dream might
fade? We'll put our hearts to-geth-er. Now we are one: I'm not a-fraid!
If there's a cloud a-bove, if it should rain we'll let it. But for to-night, for-
get it! I'm in the mood for love. love.

© 1935 (Renewed) EMI ROBBINS CATALOG INC.
All Rights Controlled by EMI ROBBINS CATALOG INC. (Publishing) and ALFRED PUBLISHING CO., INC. (Print)
All Rights Reserved

I'VE GOT A CRUSH ON YOU

Music and Lyrics by
GEORGE GERSHWIN
and IRA GERSHWIN

I'VE GOT YOU UNDER MY SKIN

Music and Lyrics by
COLE PORTER

Medium

I've got you under my skin. I've got you deep in the heart of me. So deep in my heart, you're really a part of me. I've got you under my skin. I tried so not to give in. I said to myself, "This affair never will go so well." But why should I try to resist when, darling, I know so well, I've

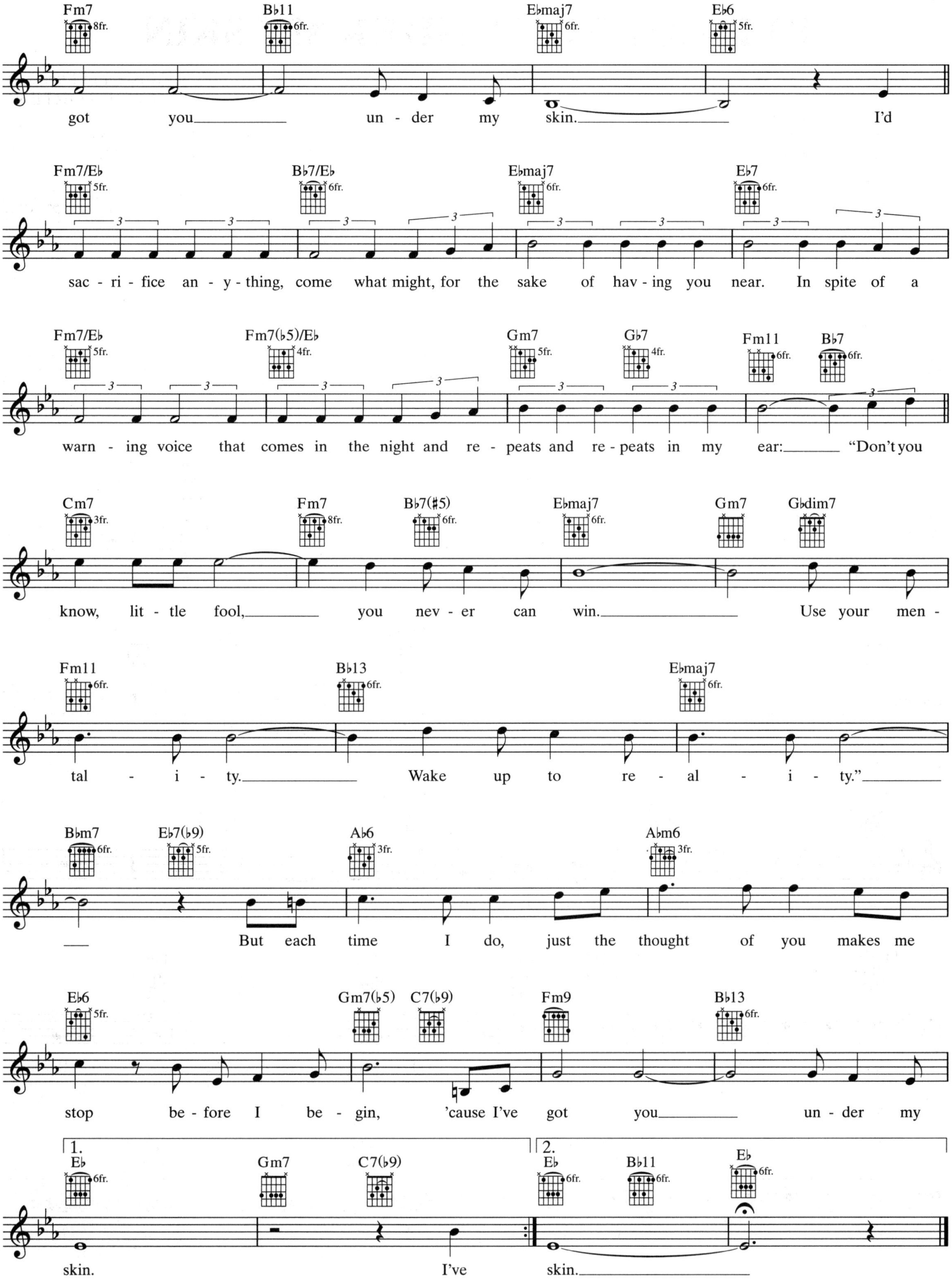

I'VE GROWN ACCUSTOMED TO HER FACE

Lyrics by ALAN J. LERNER
Music by FREDERICK LOEWE

Slow

I've grown ac - cus - tomed to her face. _____ She al - most makes the day be - gin. _____ I've grown ac - cus - tomed to the tune she whis - tles night and noon, her smiles, her frowns, her ups, her downs are sec - ond na - ture to me now; _____ like breath - ing out and breath - ing in. _____ I was se - rene - ly in - de - pen - dent and con - tent be - fore we met; sure - ly I could al - ways be that way a - gain and yet, I've grown ac - cus - tomed to her looks; ac - cus - tomed to her voice; ac - cus - tomed to her face. I've grown ac - face.

cus - tomed to her face. _____ She al - most makes the day be - gin. _____ I've got - ten used to hear her say: "Good morn - ing" ev - 'ry day, her joys, her woes, her highs, her lows are sec - ond na - ture to me now; _____ like breath - ing out and breath - ing in. _____ I'm ver - y grate - ful she's a wom - an and so eas - y to for - get; rath - er like a ha - bit one can al - ways break and yet, I've grown ac - cus - tomed to the trace of some - thing in the air; ac - cus - tomed to her

© 1956 Alan J. Lerner and Frederick Loewe
Copyright Renewed
Chappell & Co., owner of publication and allied rights throughout the World
All Rights Reserved

IT HAD TO BE YOU

Words by GUS KAHN
Music by ISHAM JONES

Freely *Chorus:*

It had to be you,_____ it had to be you._____ I wan-dered a-round and fi-nal-ly found_____ the some-bod-y who_____ could make me be true,_____ could make me be blue_____ and e-ven be glad,_____ just to be sad,_____ think-ing of you._____ Some oth-ers I've seen_____ might nev-er be mean._____ Might nev-er be cross,_____ or try to be boss,_____ but they would-n't do._____ For no-bod-y else_____ gave me a thrill._____ With all your faults,_____ I love you still._____ It had to be you,_____ won-der-ful you,_____

1. had to be you._____
2. It had to be you,_____

© 1924 (Renewed) WARNER BROS. INC.
All Rights for the Extended Term in the U.S. Controlled by
THE BANTAM MUSIC PUBLISHING CO. and GILBERT KEYES MUSIC COMPANY
All Rights Administered by WB MUSIC CORP.
All Rights Reserved

THE LADY IS A TRAMP

In strict tempo

Words by LORENZ HART
Music by RICHARD RODGERS

*Alternative version: and drifted, too

I don't like crap-games with Barons and Earls,
won't go to Harlem in ermine and pearls,
won't dish the dirt with the rest of the girls.
That's why the lady is a tramp.
I like the free, fresh wind in my hair,
life without care.
I'm broke, it's oke.
Hate California, it's cold and it's damp.
That's why the lady is a tramp.

I like a prize-fight that isn't fake.
I love the rowing on Central Park Lake.
I go to op'ra and stay wide awake.
That's why the lady is a tramp.
I like the green grass under my shoes,
what can I lose?
I'm flat! That's that!
I'm all alone when I lower my lamp.
That's why the lady is a tramp.

Refrain 3 (reprise):
Don't know the reason for cocktails at five.
I don't like flying – I'm glad I'm alive.
I crave affection, but not when I drive.
That's why the lady is a tramp.
Folks go to London and leave me behind,
I'll miss the crowning, Queen Mary won't mind.
I don't play Scarlett in Gone With The Wind.
That's why the lady is a tramp.
I like to hang my hat where I please,
Sail with the breeze.
No dough – heigh-ho!
I love La Guardia and think he's a champ.
That's why the lady is a tramp.

Refrain 4 (reprise):
Girls get massages, they cry and they moan.
Tell Lizzie Arden to leave me alone.
I'm not so hot, but my shape is my own.
That's why the lady is a tramp.
The food at Sardi's is perfect, no doubt.
I wouldn't know what the Ritz's is about.
I drop a nickel and coffee comes out.
That's why the lady is a tramp!
I like the sweet, fresh rain in my face,
Diamonds and lace,
No got – so what?
For Robert Taylor I whistle and stamp.
That's why the lady is a tramp!

The Lady Is a Tramp - 2 - 2
27526

LET'S DO IT
(Let's Fall in Love)

Music and Lyrics by
COLE PORTER

Freely *Verse:*

When the lit-tle blue-bird, who has nev-er said a word, starts to sing: "Spring, spring"; when the lit-tle blue-bell, in the bot-tom of the dell, starts to ring: "Ding, ding"; when the lit-tle blue clerk, in the mid-dle of his work, starts a tune to the moon up a-bove, it is na-ture, that's all, sim-ply tell-ing us to fall in love. And that's why

Medium *Chorus:*

birds do it, bees do it, e-ven ed-u-ca-ted fleas do it,
spon-ges, they say, do it, oy-sters down in Oy-ster Bay do it,

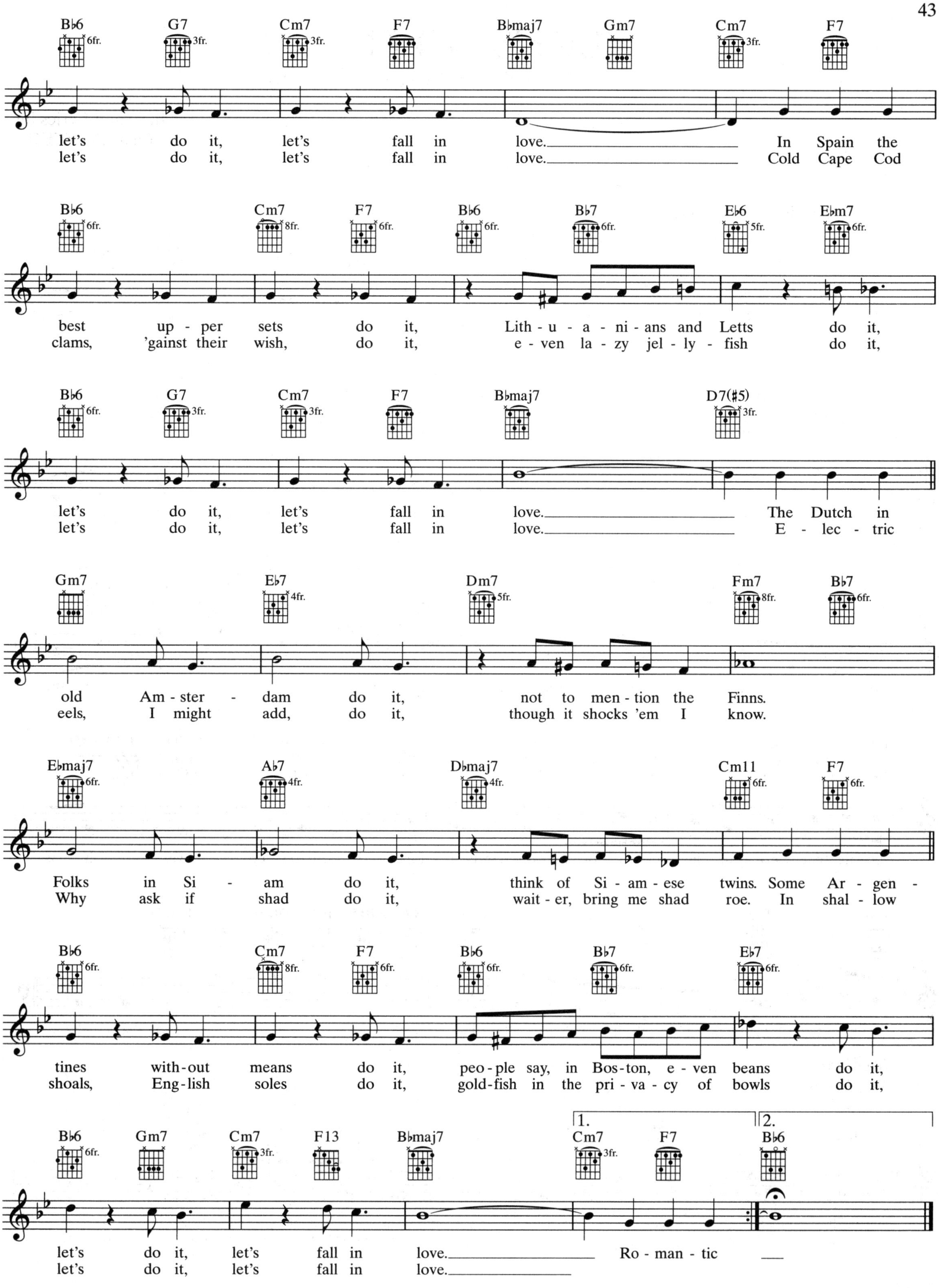

LOVE FOR SALE

Words and Music by
COLE PORTER

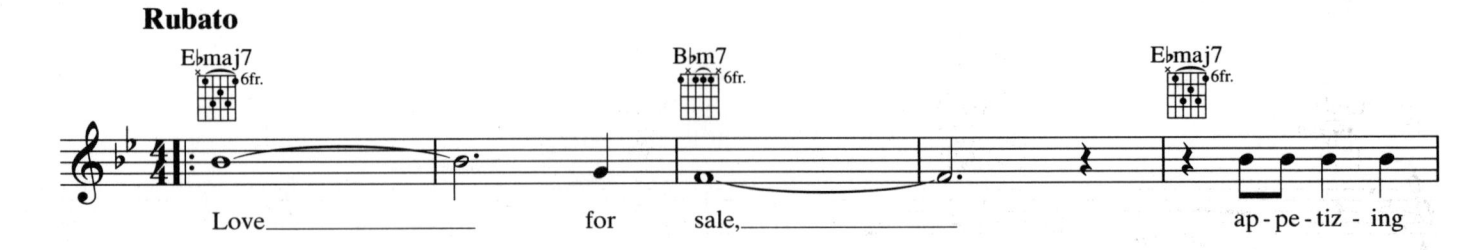

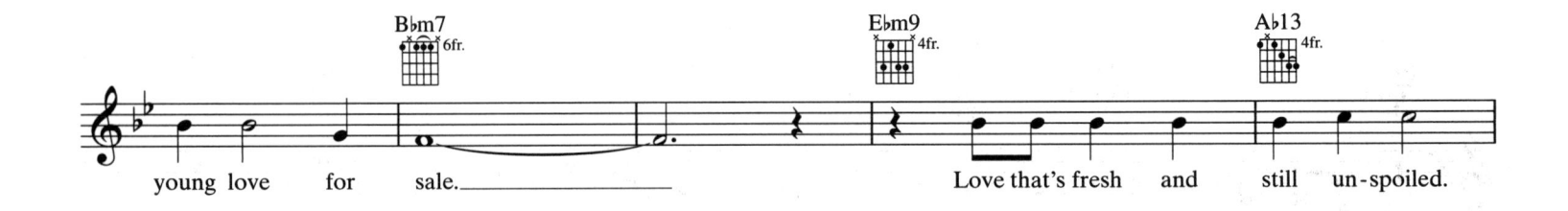

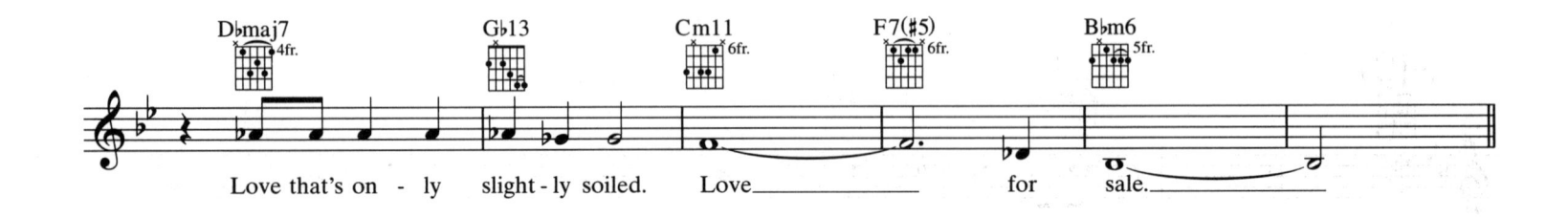

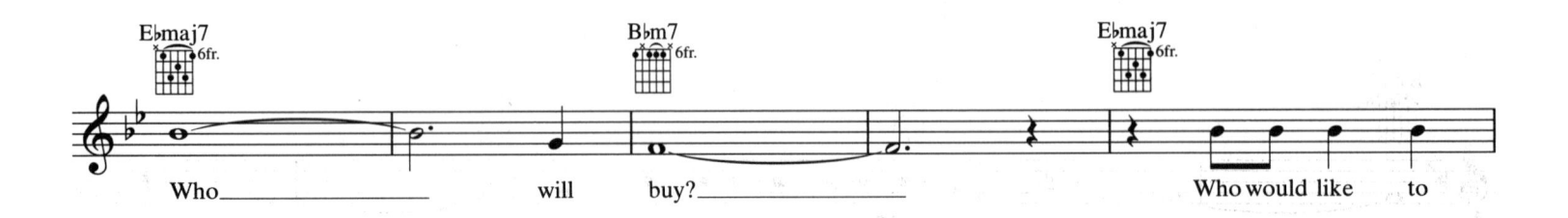

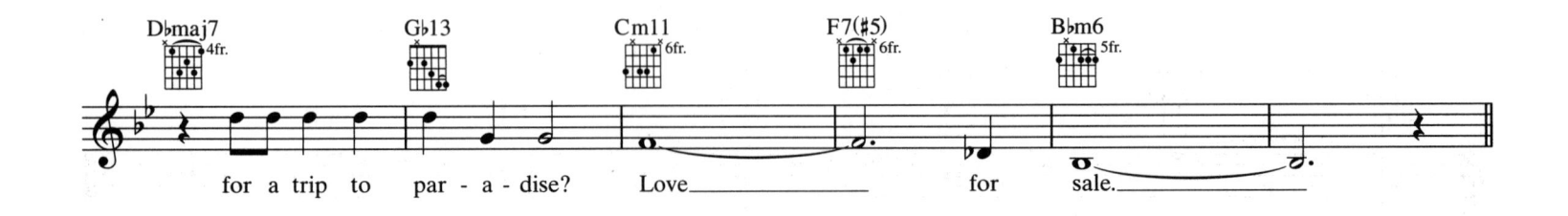

Rubato

Love_____ for sale,_____ ap-pe-tiz-ing young love for sale._____ Love that's fresh and still un-spoiled. Love that's on-ly slight-ly soiled. Love_____ for sale._____

Who_____ will buy?_____ Who would like to sam-ple my sup-ply? Who's pre-pared to pay the price for a trip to par-a-dise? Love_____ for sale._____

Love for Sale - 2 - 1
27526

© 1930 WARNER BROS. INC. (Renewed)
All Rights Reserved

Ebm7
Ab7(b9)
Dbmaj9
Fm7
Bb7(b9)
Let the po - ets pipe of love in their child - ish way.
Ebm7
Ab7(b9)
Dbmaj7
I know ev - 'ry type of love bet - ter far than they.
Bb7
B7
Bb7(b9)
Ebm7
Gm7(b5)
If you want the thrill of love I've been thru the mill of love; old love,
C7(b9 #5)
Fm7(b5)
Bb7(b9)
Ebmaj7
new love. Ev - 'ry love but true love. Love for
Bbm7
Ebmaj7
Bbm7
sale. Ap - pe - tiz - ing young love for sale.
Ebm9
Ab13
Dbmaj7
Gb13
If you want to buy my wares, fol - low me and climb the stairs.
Cm11
F7(#5)
1.
Bbm6
Bb7
2.
Bbm6
Love for sale. sale.

LAURA

Lyrics by JOHNNY MERCER
Music by DAVID RAKSIN

Ballad
Chorus:

Lau - ra is the face in the mist - y light.

Foot - steps that you hear down the hall.

The laugh that floats on a sum - mer night, that you can

nev - er quite re - call. And you see

Lau - ra on the train that is pass - ing thru.

Those eyes, how fa - mil - iar they seem. She gave

your ver - y first kiss to you. That was Lau - ra,

1. but she's on - ly a dream.

2. dream.

© 1945 (Renewed 1973) by TWENTIETH CENTURY MUSIC CORPORATION
All Rights Controlled by EMI Robbins Catalog INC. (Publishing)
and ALFRED PUBLISHING CO., INC. (Print)
All Rights Reserved

LOVE IS HERE TO STAY

Music and Lyrics by
GEORGE GERSHWIN
and IRA GERSHWIN

Moderate swing *Chorus:*

It's ve-ry clear our love is here to stay; not for a year but ev-er and a day. The ra-di-o and the tel-e-phone and the mov-ies that we know may just be pass-ing fan-cies, and in time may go. But, oh my dear, our love is here to stay; to-geth-er we're go-ing a long, long way. In time the Rock-ies may crum-ble, Gib-ral-tar may tum-ble, they're on-ly made of clay, but our love is

1. here to stay._____ It's ve-ry

2. stay._____

© 1938 (Renewed 1965) GEORGE GERSHWIN MUSIC and IRA GERSHWIN MUSIC
All Rights Administered by WB MUSIC CORP.
All Rights Reserved

MOONGLOW

Words and Music by
WILL HUDSON, EDDIE DELANGE
and IRVING MILLS

Slow/med.

It must have been moon-glow, way up in the blue,
it must have been moon-glow that led me straight to you.
I still hear you say-ing, 'Dear one, hold me fast.'
And I start in pray-ing, 'Oh Lord, please let this last.'
We seemed to float right through the air.
Heav-en-ly songs seemed to come from ev-'ry-where.
And now when there's moon-glow, way up in the blue,
I al-ways re-mem-ber

1. that moon-glow gave me you.
2. that moon-glow gave me you.

© 1934 (Renewed 1962) and Assigned to EMI MILLS MUSIC, INC. and SCARSDALE MUSIC CORPORATION
All Rights Reserved

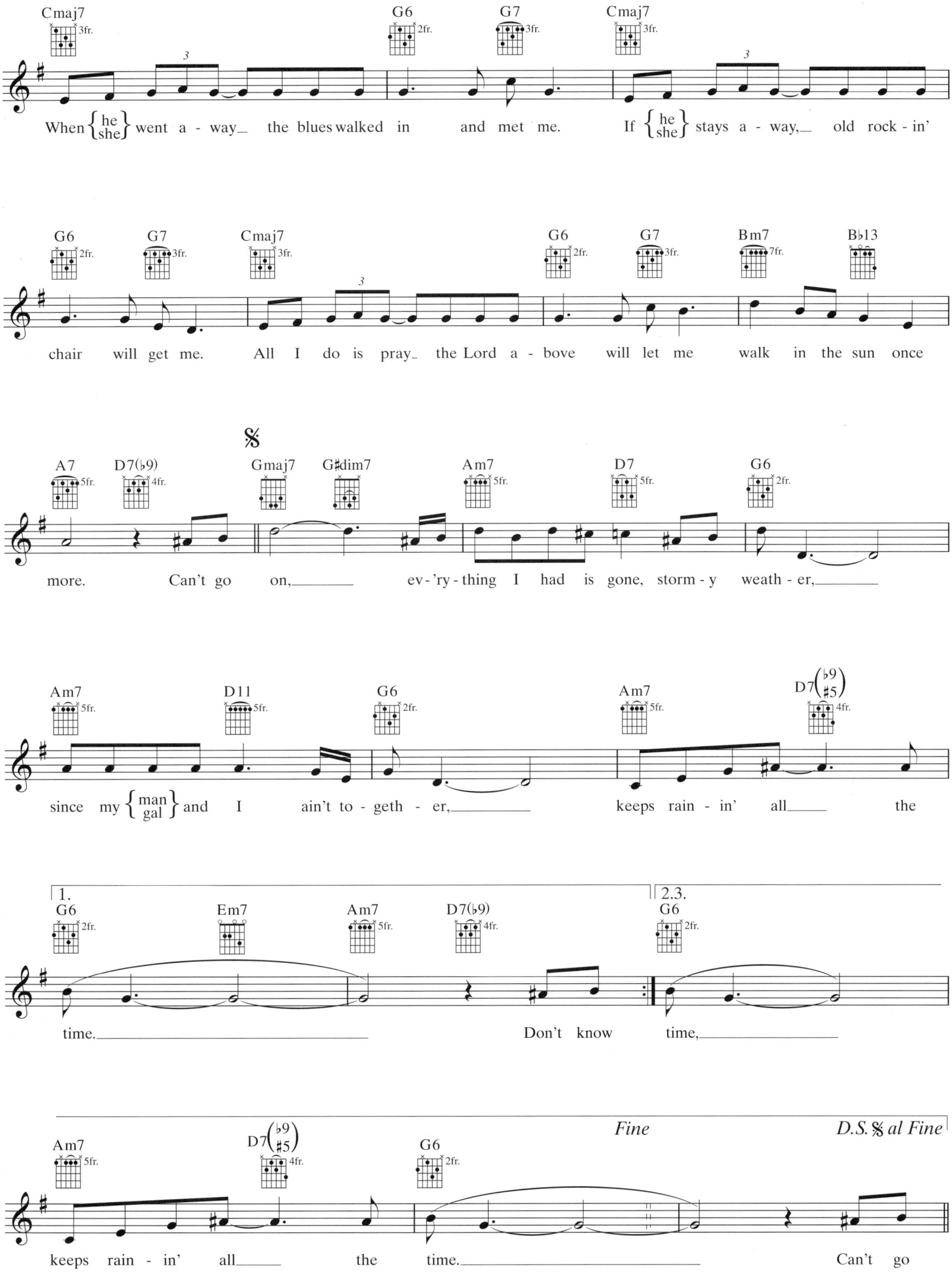
Cmaj7 G6 G7 Cmaj7
When {he/she} went a - way_ the blues walked in and met me. If {he/she} stays a - way,_ old rock - in'
G6 G7 Cmaj7 G6 G7 Bm7 B♭13
chair will get me. All I do is pray_ the Lord a - bove will let me walk in the sun once
A7 D7(♭9) Gmaj7 G♯dim7 Am7 D7 G6
more. Can't go on,_ ev - 'ry - thing I had is gone, storm - y weath - er,_
Am7 D11 G6 Am7 D7(♭9 ♯5)
since my {man/gal} and I ain't to - geth - er,_ keeps rain - in' all_ the
1. G6 Em7 Am7 D7(♭9) 2.3. G6
time._ Don't know time,_
Am7 D7(♭9 ♯5) G6 Fine D.S. al Fine
keeps rain - in' all_ the time._ Can't go

SOMEONE TO WATCH OVER ME

Music and Lyrics by
GEORGE GERSHWIN
and IRA GERSHWIN

Moderately
Chorus:

SUMMER WIND

English Words by JOHNNY MERCER
Original German Lyrics by HANS BRADTKE
Music by HENRY MAYER

Slow

1. The sum-mer wind came blow-ing in a-cross the sea, it lin-gered there to touch your hair and walk with me. All sum-mer long we sang a song and strolled the gold-en sand, two sweet-hearts and the sum-mer wind.

2. Like painted kites, the days and nights went fly-ing by, the world was new be-neath a blue um-brel-la sky. Then soft-er than a pip-er man one day it called to you, I lost you to the sum-mer wind.

3. The au-tumn wind, the win-ter winds have come and gone, and still the days, the lone-ly days go on and on. And guess who sighs his lul-la-bies through nights that nev-er end, my fick-le friend, the sum-mer wind.

© 1965 EDITION PRIMUS Rolf Budde KG © 1965 WARNER BROS. INC.
Copyrights Renewed
All Rights Reserved

THEY CAN'T TAKE THAT AWAY FROM ME

Music and Lyrics by
GEORGE GERSHWIN
and IRA GERSHWIN

Freely

The way you wear your hat, the way you sip your tea,

the mem-r'y of all that,

no, no! They can't take that a-way from me! The way your smile just beams,

the way you sing off key,

the way you haunt my dreams, no, no! They

can't take that a-way from me. We may nev-er, nev-er

They Can't Take That Away From Me - 2 - 1
27526

© 1936, 1937 (Renewed 1963, 1964) GEORGE GERSHWIN MUSIC and IRA GERSHWIN MUSIC
All Rights Administered by WB MUSIC CORP.
All Rights Reserved

Gm7 Am7(♭5) D7(♭9) Gm7 Em7(♭5) A7 Am11 D7
meet a - gain on the bump - y road to love. Still I'll
Gm7 Am7(♭5) D7(♭9) Gm7 C7 F7
al - ways, al - ways keep the mem - r'y of
A♭/B♭ E♭6 E♭maj7 E♭/G G♭dim7
the way you hold your knife, the way we danced till three,
Fm7 A♭/B♭ B♭m7
the way you've changed my life,
E♭7 A♭maj7 Fm7 B♭7 Cm7 Fm7(♭5)
no, no! They can't take that a - way from me! No, they
E♭/B♭ Fm7/B♭ B♭13 1. E♭
can't take that a - way from me!
A♭/B♭ 2. E♭ E♭6
The way you wear your hat, me!

WHAT A WONDERFUL WORLD

Words and Music by
GEORGE DAVID WEISS
and BOB THIELE

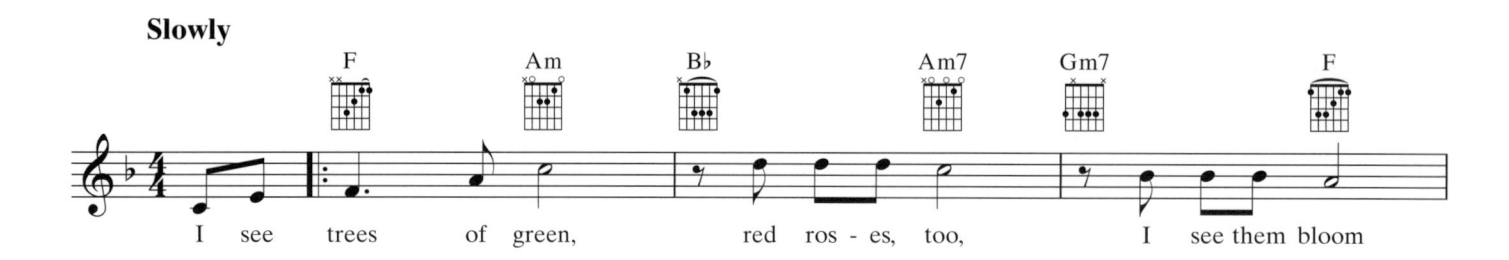

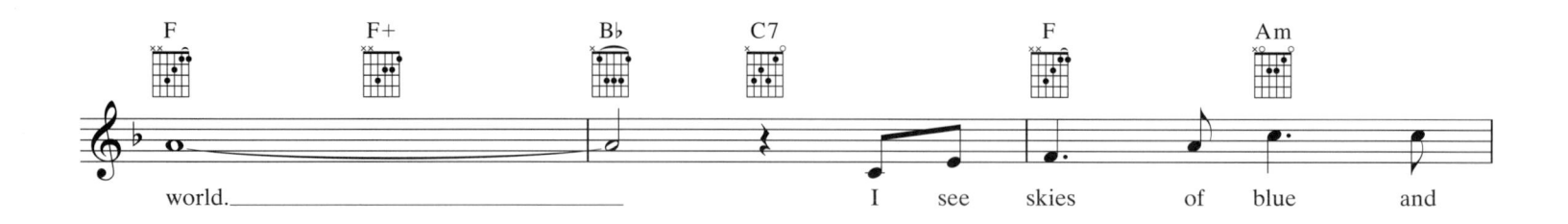

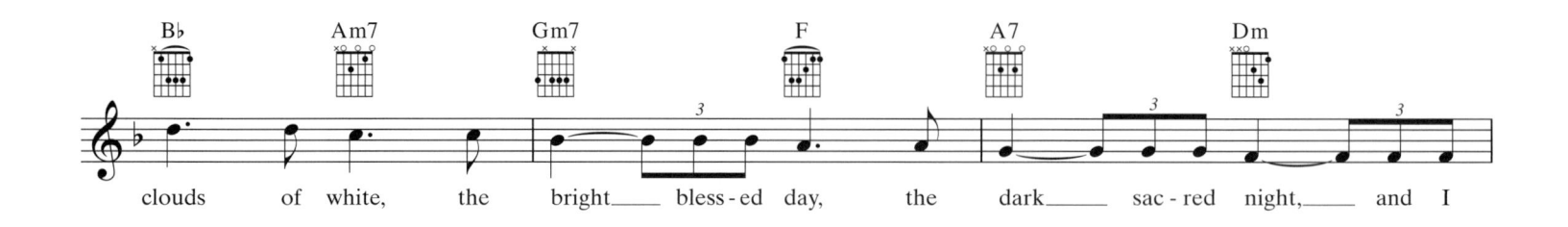

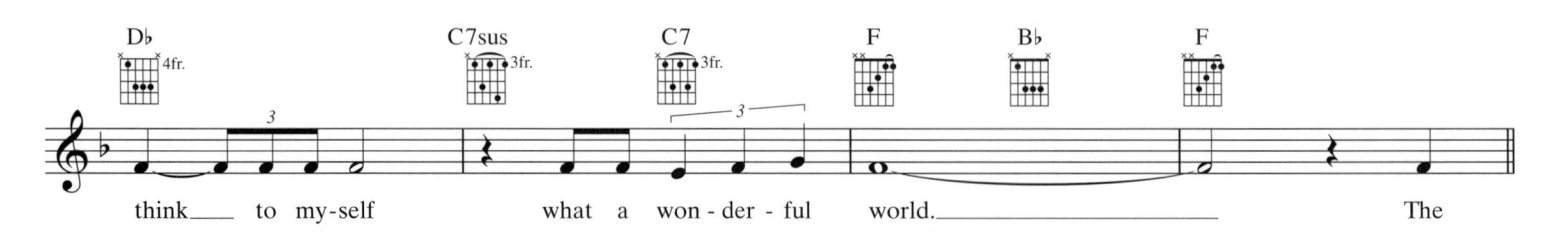

Slowly

I see trees of green, red ros-es, too, I see them bloom for me and you, and I think to my-self what a won-der-ful world. I see skies of blue and clouds of white, the bright bless-ed day, the dark sac-red night, and I think to my-self what a won-der-ful world. The

© 1967 RANGE ROAD MUSIC INC. and QUARTET MUSIC INC.
© Renewed 1995 by GEORGE DAVID WEISS and BOB THIELE
Rights for GEORGE DAVID WEISS Assigned to ABILENE MUSIC, INC.
and Administered by THE SONGWRITERS GUILD OF AMERICA
All Rights Reserved

C7 3fr. F C7 3fr.
col - ors of the rain - bow, so pret - ty in the sky are al - so on the fac - es of
F Dm C Dm C
peo - ple go - in' by. I see friends shak - in' hands, say - in', "How do you do!"
Dm F♯dim7 Gm7 F♯dim7 Gm7 C7 F Am
They're real - ly say - in,' "I love you." I hear ba - bies cry, I
B♭ Am7 Gm7 F A7 Dm
watch them grow. They'll learn much more than I'll ev - er know, and I
D♭ 4fr. C7sus 3fr. C7 3fr. F Am7(♭5)/E♭
think to my - self what a won - der - ful world.
D7 Gm7 Gm7/C C7(♭9)
Yes, I think to my - self what a won - der - ful
1. F Dm7 Gm7 C7
world. I see
2. F B♭ F
world.
3
3fr.

SUMMERTIME

By GEORGE GERSHWIN,
DuBOSE and DOROTHY HEYWARD
and IRA GERSHWIN

Slowly

Sum-mer-time____ and the liv-in' is eas-y.____ Fish are jump-in'____ and the cot-ton is high.____ Oh, your dad-dy's rich____ and your ma-ma's good look-in'.____ So hush, lit-tle ba-by, don't____ you cry.____ One of these morn-in's you're goin' to rise____ up sing-in', then you'll spread your wings____ and you'll take to the sky.____ But till that morn-in'____ there's-a noth-in' can harm you____ with Dad-dy and Mam-my stand-in' by.____

© 1935 (Renewed 1962) GEORGE GERSHWIN MUSIC, IRA GERSHWIN MUSIC
and DuBOSE and DOROTHY HEYWARD MEMORIAL FUND
All Rights Administered by WB MUSIC CORP.
All Rights Reserved

WHAT'S NEW?

Words by JOHNNY BURKE
Music by BOB HAGGART

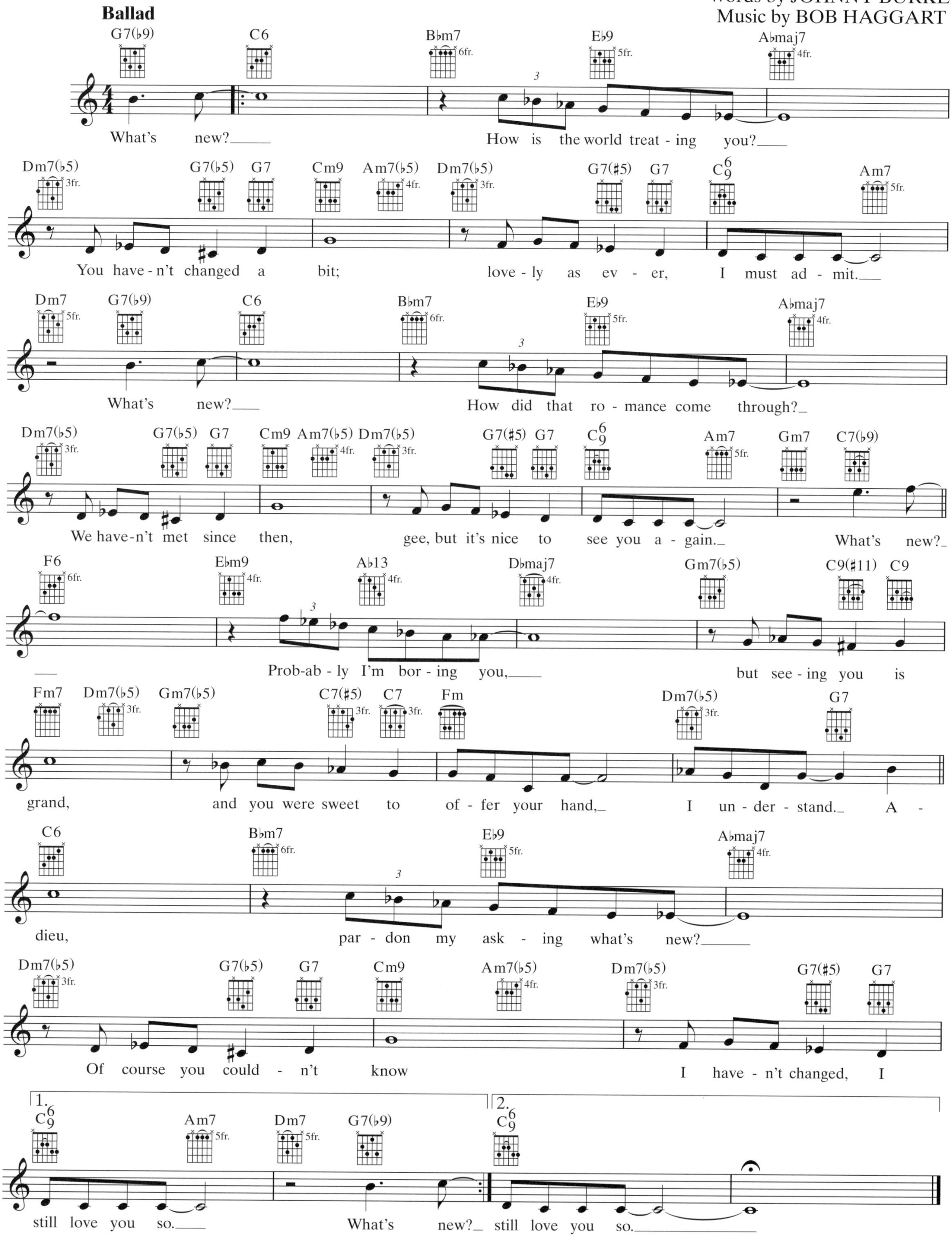

WHERE OR WHEN

Words by LORENZ HART
Music by RICHARD RODGERS

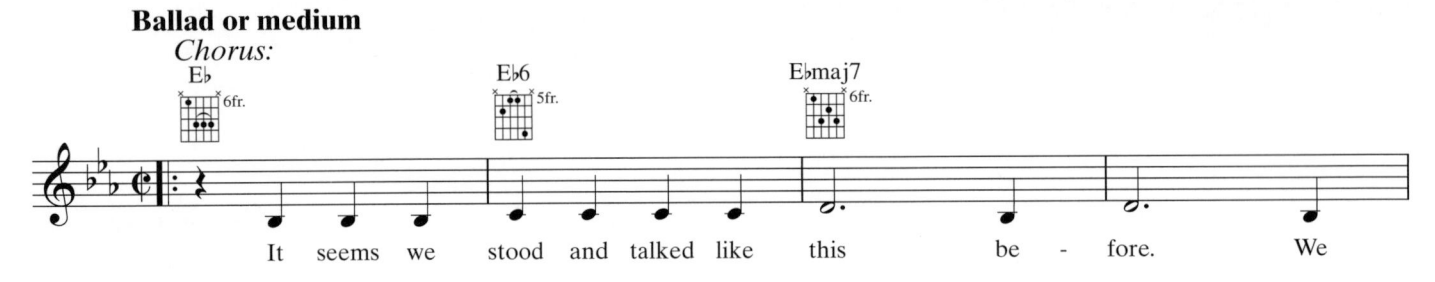

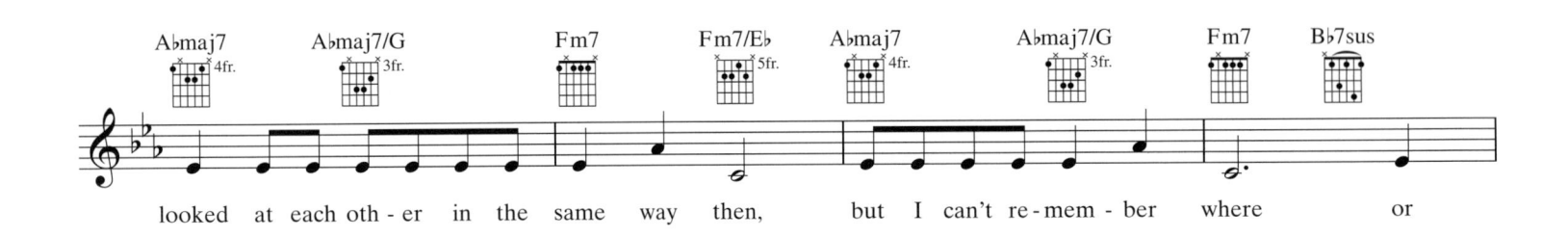

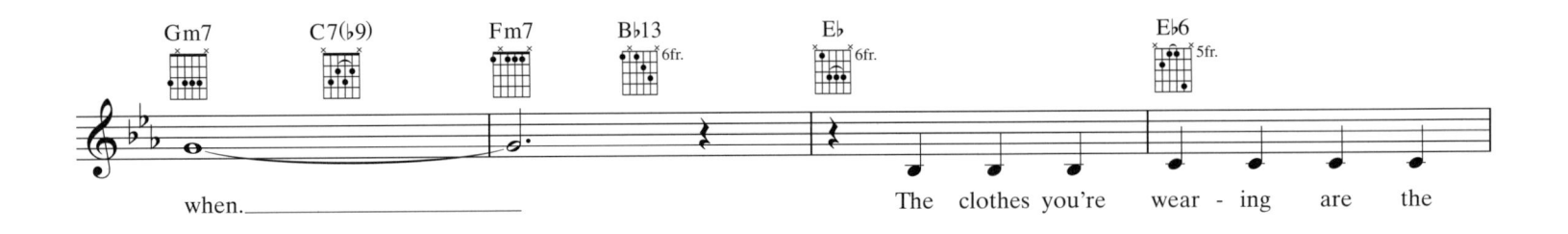

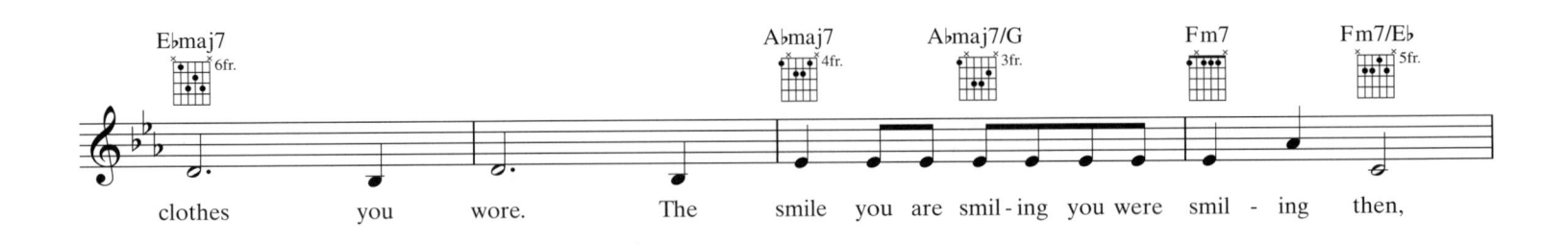

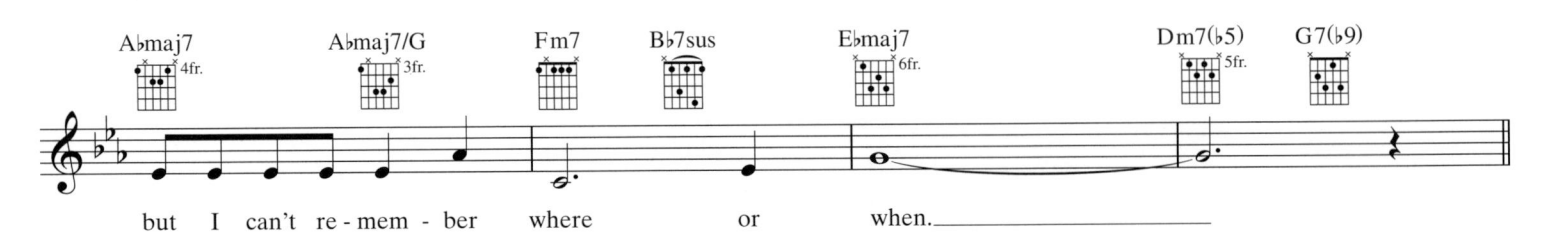

Ballad or medium
Chorus:

It seems we stood and talked like this be-fore. We looked at each oth-er in the same way then, but I can't re-mem-ber where or when. The clothes you're wear-ing are the clothes you wore. The smile you are smil-ing you were smil-ing then, but I can't re-mem-ber where or when.

Where or When - 2 - 1
27526

© 1937 (Renewed) CHAPPELL & CO.
Rights for Extended Renewal Term in the U.S. Administered by WB MUSIC CORP. and WILLIAMSON MUSIC
All Rights Reserved

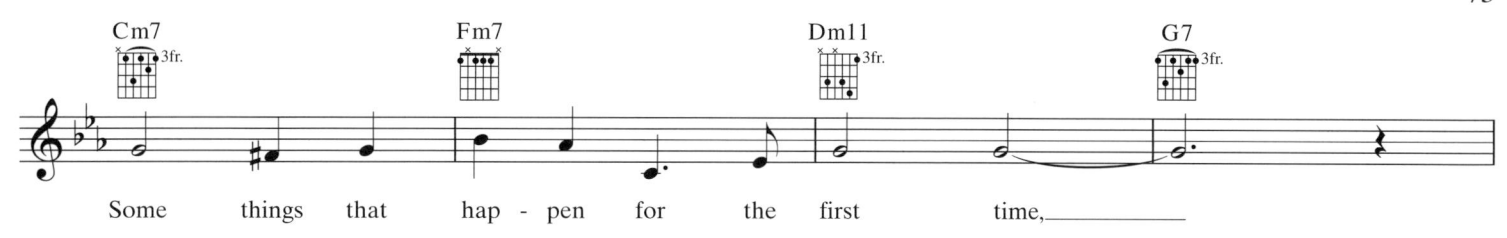

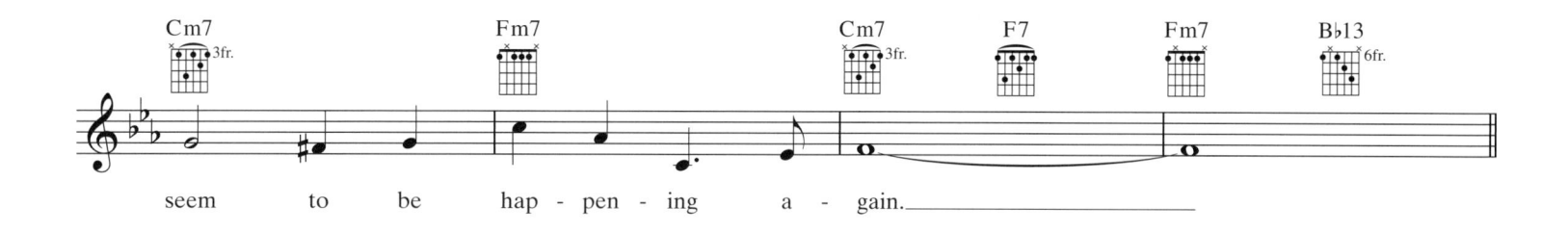

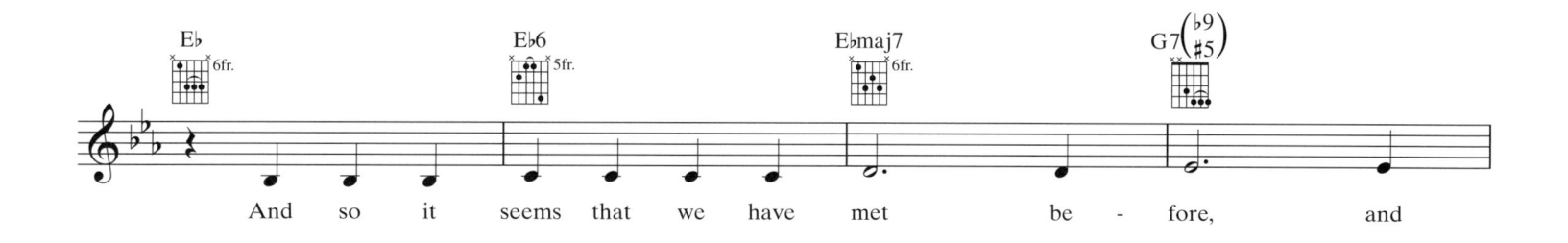

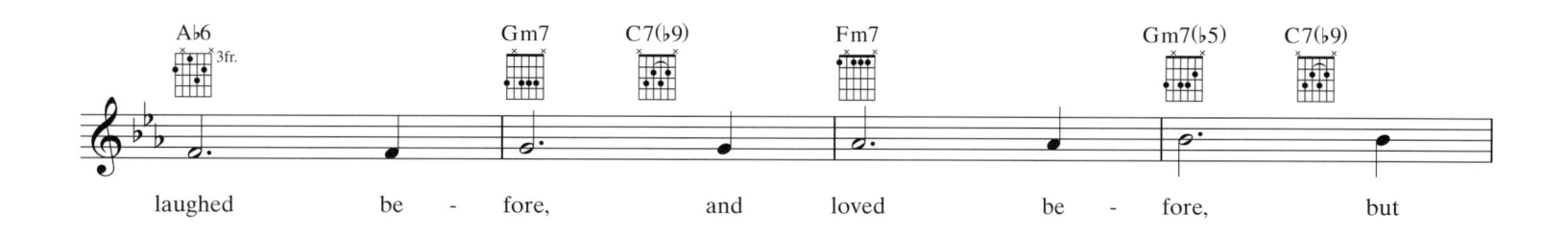

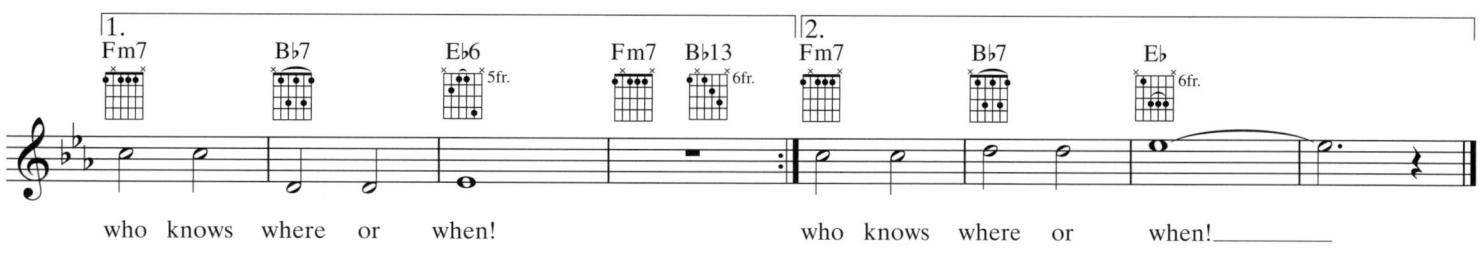

Some things that hap-pen for the first time,

seem to be hap-pen-ing a-gain.

And so it seems that we have met be-fore, and

laughed be-fore, and loved be-fore, but

1. who knows where or when!

2. who knows where or when!

Where or When - 2 - 2
27526

YOU GO TO MY HEAD

Words by HAVEN GILLESPIE
Music by J. FRED COOTS

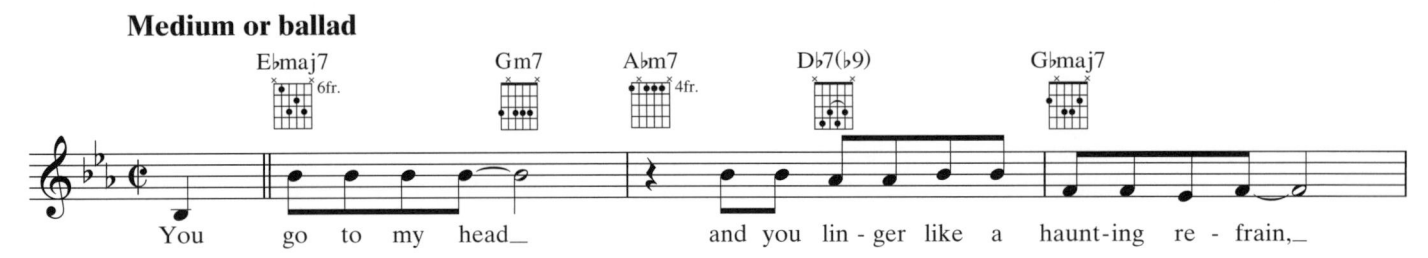

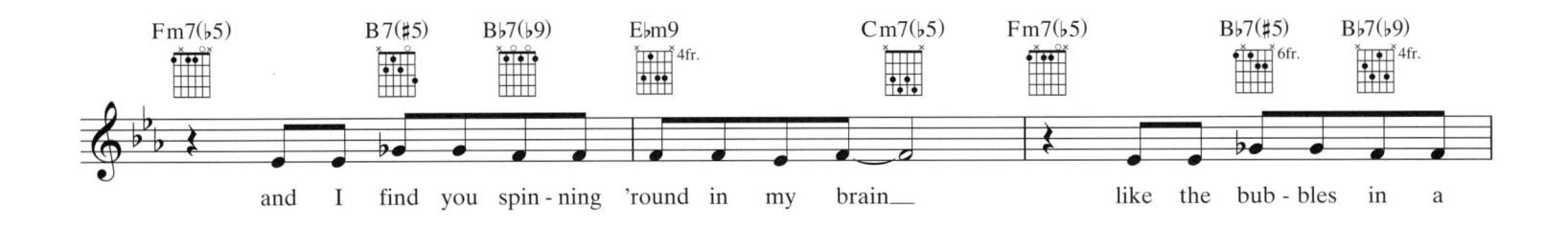

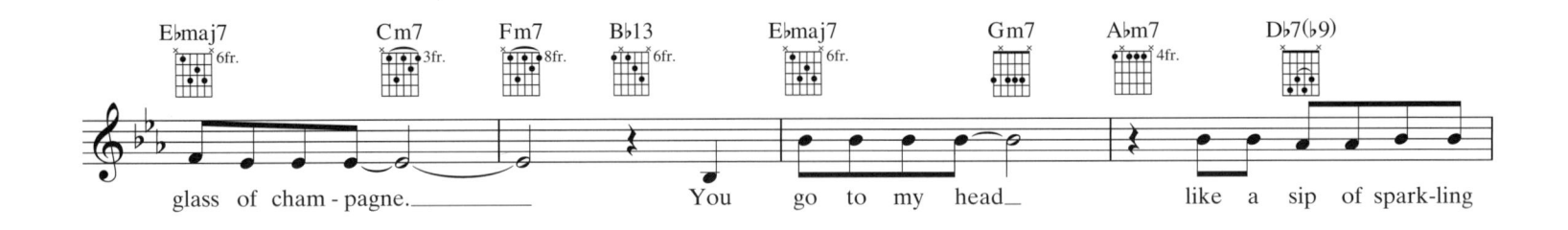

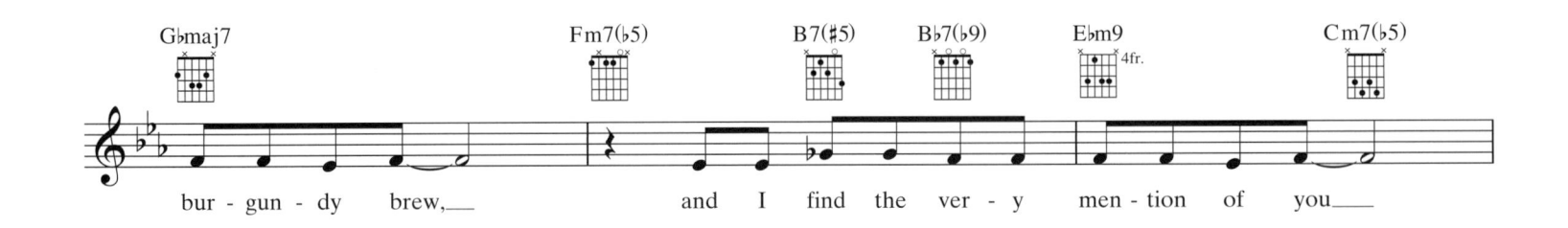

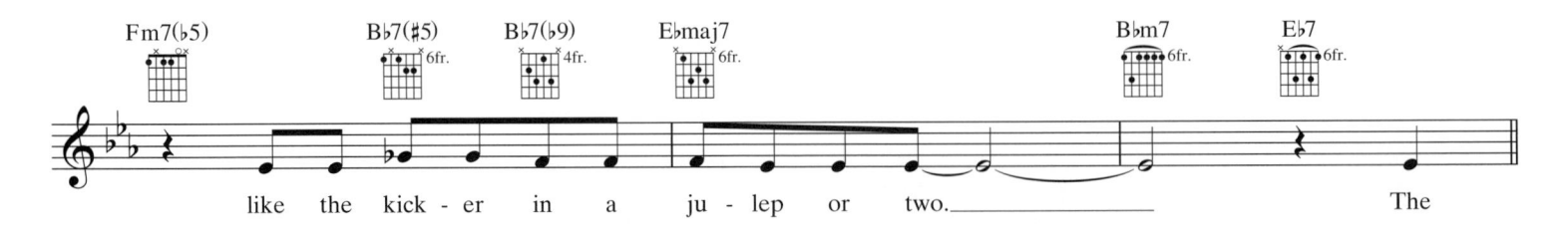

Medium or ballad

| Ebmaj7 | Gm7 | Abm7 | Db7(b9) | Gbmaj7 |

You go to my head___ and you lin-ger like a haunt-ing re-frain,___

| Fm7(b5) | B7(#5) | Bb7(b9) | Ebm9 | Cm7(b5) | Fm7(b5) | Bb7(#5) | Bb7(b9) |

and I find you spin-ning 'round in my brain___ like the bub-bles in a

| Ebmaj7 | Cm7 | Fm7 | Bb13 | Ebmaj7 | Gm7 | Abm7 | Db7(b9) |

glass of cham-pagne.___ You go to my head___ like a sip of spark-ling

| Gbmaj7 | Fm7(b5) | B7(#5) | Bb7(b9) | Ebm9 | Cm7(b5) |

bur-gun-dy brew,___ and I find the ver-y men-tion of you___

| Fm7(b5) | Bb7(#5) | Bb7(b9) | Ebmaj7 | Bbm7 | Eb7 |

like the kick-er in a ju-lep or two.___ The

You Go to My Head - 2 - 1
27526

© 1938 (Renewed) TOY TOWN TUNES, INC. and HAVEN GILLESPIE MUSIC PUBL. CO.
All Rights on behalf of TOY TOWN TUNES, INC. Administered by WB MUSIC CORP.
All Rights Reserved

thrill of the thought that you might give a thought to my plea casts a spell o-ver me.

Still I say to my-self, "Get a hold of your-self, can't you

see that it nev-er can be." You go to my head

with a smile that makes my tem-p'ra-ture rise, like a sum-mer with a

thou-sand Ju-lys, you in-tox-i-cate my soul with your eyes.

Tho' I'm cer-tain that this heart of mine

has-n't a ghost of a chance in this cra-zy ro-mance,

you go to my head.

WHEN I FALL IN LOVE

Words by EDWARD HEYMAN
Music by VICTOR YOUNG

Med. ballad

Chorus:

When I fall in love, it will be for-ev-er, or I'll nev-er fall in love. In a rest-less world like this is, love is end-ed be-fore it's be-gun, and too man-y moon-light kiss-es seem to cool in the warmth of the sun. When I give my heart, it will be com-plete-ly, or I'll nev-er give my heart. And the mo-ment I can feel that you feel that way too, is

1. when I fall in love with you.
2. you.

© 1952 by VICTOR YOUNG PUBLICATIONS, INC.
Copyright Renewed, Assigned to CHAPPELL & CO. and INTERSONG - USA, INC.
All Rights Administered by CHAPPELL & CO.
All Rights Reserved

THE Just Real

Collect Them All!

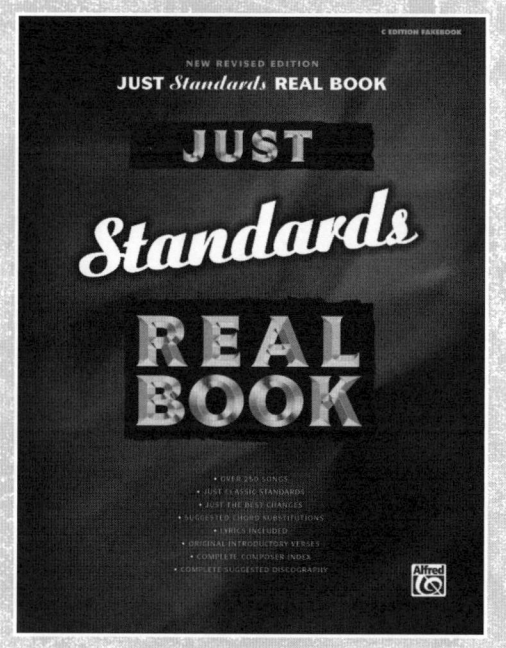

FBM0002A

- OVER 250 SONGS
- JUST CLASSIC STANDARDS
- JUST THE BEST CHANGES
- SUGGESTED CHORD SUBSTITUTIONS
- LYRICS INCLUDED
- ORIGINAL INTRODUCTORY VERSES
- COMPLETE COMPOSER INDEX
- COMPLETE SUGGESTED DISCOGRAPHY

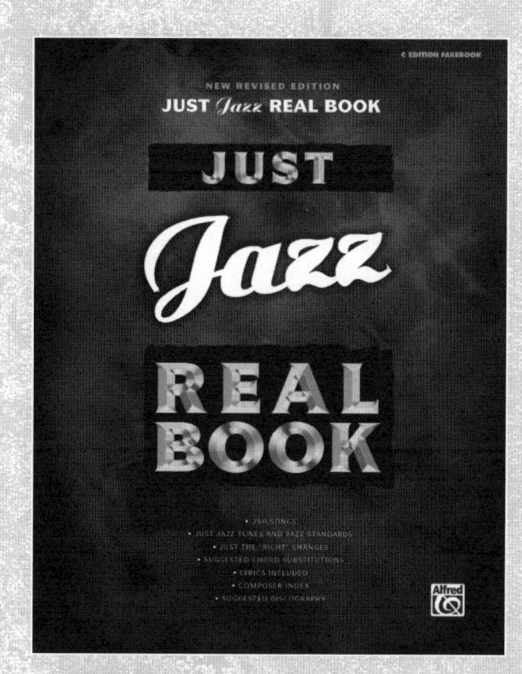

FBM0003

- 250 SONGS
- JUST JAZZ TUNES AND JAZZ STANDARDS
- JUST THE BEST CHANGES
- SUGGESTED CHORD SUBSTITUTIONS
- LYRICS INCLUDED
- COMPOSER INDEX
- SUGGESTED DISCOGRAPHY

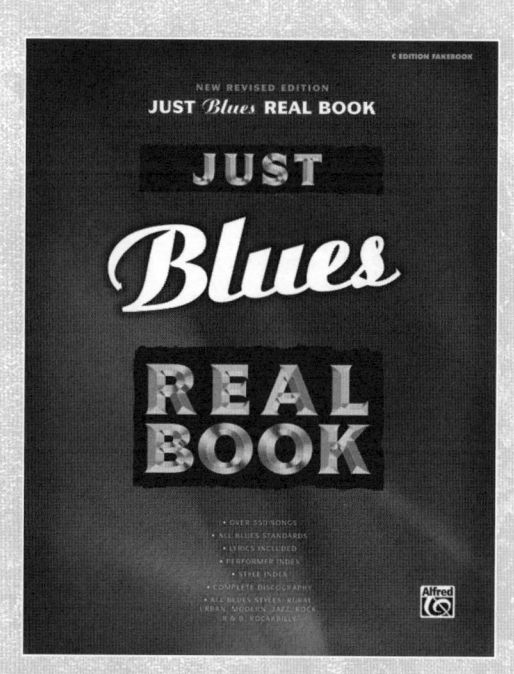

FBM0004

- OVER 350 SONGS
- ALL BLUES STANDARDS
- LYRICS INCLUDED
- PERFORMER INDEX
- STYLE INDEX
- COMPLETE DISCOGRAPHY
- ALL BLUES STYLES: RURAL, URBAN, MODERN, JAZZ, ROCK, R & B, ROCKABILLY

BOOK SERIES

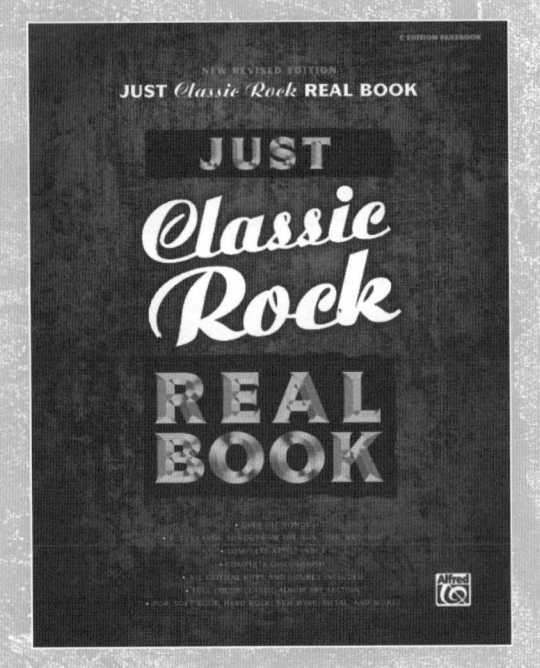

FBM0005A

- OVER 215 SONGS
- JUST CLASSIC SONGS FROM THE '60S, '70S, AND '80S
- COMPLETE ARTIST INDEX
- COMPLETE DISCOGRAPHY
- ALL CRITICAL RIFFS AND FIGURES INCLUDED
- POP, SOFT ROCK, HARD ROCK, NEW WAVE, METAL, AND MORE!

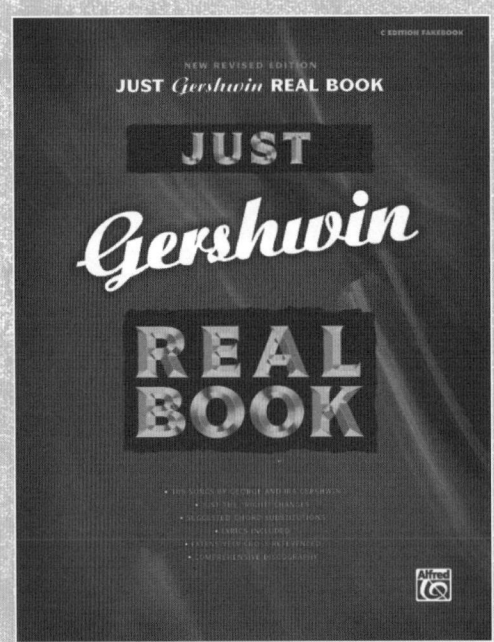

FBM0006

- 109 SONGS BY GEORGE AND IRA GERSHWIN
- JUST THE BEST CHANGES
- SUGGESTED CHORD SUBSTITUTIONS
- LYRICS INCLUDED
- EXTENSIVELY CROSS-REFERENCED
- COMPREHENSIVE DISCOGRAPHY

FBM0007

- PHOTO GALLERY
- ALL CRITICAL RIFFS AND FIGURES INCLUDED
- SELECTED RIFFS SECTION IN FULL GUITAR TAB
- SELECTED SOLOS SECTION IN FULL GUITAR TAB
- ALL SONGS FROM: LED ZEPPELIN, LED ZEPPELIN II, LED ZEPPELIN III, (IV), HOUSES OF THE HOLY, PHYSICAL GRAFFITI, PRESENCE, IN THROUGH THE OUT DOOR, CODA